OPTIMIZE YOUR AIRBNB

The Definitive Guide to RANKING #1 in AIRBNB Search

DANIEL V. RUSTEEN

Former Airbnb Employee

Creator of OptimizeMyAirbnb.com

Supercharge your listing by visiting: www.OptimizeMyAirbnb.com

Book website: www.OptimizeYOURAirbnb.com

First edition: January 2018

ISBN 978-0-9997155-0-5

Table of Contents

Reader Bonus vii

Hyperlinks viii

Disclaimer ix

Foreword by Symon He   *(Reading Time: 2 Minutes)* xi

Introduction   *(Reading Time: 2 Minutes)* 1

About the Author   *(Reading Time: 6 Minutes)* 4

Airbnb Explained in 120 Words   *(Reading Time: 1 Minute)* 10

About Airbnb, an Insider's Perspective   *(Reading Time: 12 Minutes)* 11

PART I: YOUR ONLINE AIRBNB LISTING

Chapter 1: Snappy, Catchy, + Thorough: Your Airbnb
   Listings Mantra
   (Reading Time: 3 Minutes) 21

Chapter 2: Use Your Phone to Take Better Photos
   (Reading Time: 18 Minutes) 24

Chapter 3: 5 Photo Tips for More Reservations
   (Reading Time: 6 Minutes) 36

Chapter 4: Mastering the Title
   (Reading Time: 6 Minutes) 42

Chapter 5: Mastering the Text
   (Reading Time: 4 Minutes) 50

Chapter 6: 17 Unconventional Ways to Increase Your Search Rank

(Reading Time: 14 Minutes) 54

Chapter 7: Pro Tip: 3 Pros + 2 Cons

(Reading Time: 3 Minutes) 61

Chapter 8: Pricing Hack for More Views

(Reading Time: 8 Minutes) 64

Chapter 9: Let's Talk About Revenue Management

(Reading Time: 8 Minutes) 68

Chapter 10: Why You Should Respond to Guest Reviews + How

(Reading Time: 2 Minutes) 72

Chapter 11: How to Re-Optimize Your Listing

(Reading Time: 8 Minutes) 75

PART II: YOUR OFFLINE HOSTING STYLE

Chapter 12: 5 Tips to 5-Star Reviews

(Reading Time: 10 Minutes) 81

Chapter 13: Superhost Checklist

(Reading Time: 19 Minutes) 86

Chapter 14: Interior Design Tips

(Reading Time: 9 Minutes) 95

Chapter 15: Turning Your Space into a Pet-Friendly Listing

(Reading Time: 3 Minutes) 99

Chapter 16: Make Your Airbnb Event Ready

(Reading Time: 5 Minutes) 102

Chapter 17: Cleaning Team Checklist

(Reading Time: 10 Minutes) 107

PART III: YOUR ONLINE HOSTING STYLE

Chapter 18: Optimizing + Automating Your Messages

(Reading Time: 14 Minutes) 115

Chapter 19: Calendar Strategy for New Listings
(Reading Time: 7 Minutes). 123

Chapter 20: Improve Your Airbnb Profile for More Guests
(Reading Time: 5 Minutes). 126

Chapter 21: How to Complete 100% of Your Host Profile
(Reading Time: 9 Minutes). 129

Chapter 22: What to Do When a Guest Asks to Book Offline
(Reading Time: 4 Minutes). 135

Chapter 23: Why You Should Only List on One Vacation
Rental Platform
(Reading Time: 3 Minutes). 139

PART IV: COMPANY + BOOK REVIEWS

Chapter 24: Smartbnb Review + Guide, Message Automation
(Reading Time: 11 Minutes) 147

Chapter 25: PriceLabs, Smart Pricing Tool
(Reading Time: 15 Minutes) 153

Chapter 26: Payfully, Payment Advancement
(Reading Time: 4 Minutes). 163

Chapter 27: Hostfully Review, Electronic Guidebook
(Reading Time: 5 Minutes). 166

Chapter 28: NoiseAware + Party Squasher Review, Noise
Monitoring
(Reading Time: 5 Minutes). 171

Chapter 29: Book Reviews
(Reading Time: 3 Minutes). 174

PART V: BONUS CONTENT

Chapter 30: How to Put Your Airbnb on Autopilot
(Reading Time: 12 Minutes) 181

Chapter 31: 17 Ways to Improve Your Hosting
(Reading Time: 10 Minutes) 187

Chapter 32: How to Identify Problem Guests Before They Book
(Reading Time: 14 Minutes) 192

Chapter 33: How to Write a Proper Review
(Reading Time: 3 Minutes) 200

Chapter 34: Slow Season Strategies
(Reading Time: 12 Minutes) 203

Chapter 35: Creating Additional Revenue Streams
(Reading Time: 7 Minutes) 209

Chapter 36: How Safe Is Airbnb?
(Reading Time: 7 Minutes) 212

Chapter 37: Airbnb Host Insurance Information
(Reading Time: 7 Minutes) 218

Chapter 38: Q+A with Darren Pettyjohn of Proper Insure
(Reading Time: 11 Minutes) 224

Chapter 39: Five Ways to Contact Airbnb
(Reading Time: 4 Minutes) 230

Chapter 40: Useful Airbnb Links
(Reading Time: 10 Minutes) 233

Final Notes   *(Reading Time: 1 Minute)* 237

Reader Bonus

As a thank-you for purchasing, I'd like to offer you a bundle of free goodies.

- In Chapter 17: Cleaning Team Checklist, I provide you the same Cleaning Team Checklist for sale on my website for $20. If you'd like the Word format, you can download it at the link below.
- You will also receive a PDF containing all discounts available to OptimizeMyAirbnb.com purchasers. This comes out to over $300 in discounts from 14 companies.
- Additionally, I am extending a 50% discount to my Airbnb Message Flow Strategy + Templates product as it relates to Chapter 18: Optimizing and Automating Your Messages. See chapter for discount code.

**Download your bonus items by clicking
'Claim Bonus' at www.OptimizeYourAirbnb.com**

Hyperlinks

All of the links contained in this book are added for the readers benefit. Some are affiliate links. An affiliate link means that I earn a small commission (at no cost to you) if you make a purchase. Some of the links contain an automatic discount upon purchase. I invested 350+ hours creating this book and decided to leverage this additional revenue stream. I hope that you are ok with this. If not, simply search the product or company without clicking the link. I don't recommend anything I don't use unless specified.

Disclaimer

All opinions and advice in this book are solely those of the author, provided "as-is", and do not reflect the opinion of Airbnb. The author has no relationship with Airbnb. This book is for educational purposes only. Care has been taken to ensure the information in this book is true and correct as of the time of publication. Any changes to the Airbnb platform made after the time of publication may impact the accuracy of the information contained herein. The author assumes no liability of any kind with respect to the completeness or accuracy of the contents. The author cannot be held liable or responsible to any person or entity with respect to any loss or incidental or consequential damages caused by or alleged to have been caused directly or indirectly by the information contained herein. The author does not offer professional advice as it related to legal, accounting, or any other service.

Foreword

by Symon He
from LearnAirbnb

There are few times in your life when a conversation stays with you. The first time I spoke to Danny Rusteen was one of those times. We talked about Airbnb host strategies and tactics, the conversation was a one-way download of Airbnb hosting insights from him to me. Understanding new ideas from other people isn't something new for me; I learn new things from every conversation. However, in the context of Airbnb hosting insights, the conversation surprised me.

• • •

Rusteen showcases how every choice you make as a host impacts your time, your profits, and your experience.

• • •

When Rusteen and I first met, I had recently completed a research study analyzing Airbnb data of over 250,000 hosts and 400,000 listings across 200 major markets. I had also finished a detailed attitudinal survey of 1,300 hosts at various levels of experience. I had an insight into Airbnb even the most experienced hosts don't have. And through my blog LearnAirbnb.com, I regularly crowd sourced and pulled hosting strategies from over 150,000 hosts every month.

Furthermore, I have personally coached thousands of new and experienced hosts over the past five years. I've helped new Airbnb hosts complete their listings, land their first booking, and become Superhosts.

I've even helped some hosts grow their Airbnb empire from one listing to dozens of listings (including one with over 500 listings).

So when it comes to Airbnb hosting strategies and tactics, I'm usually the one providing insights. However, when I first met Rusteen, it was the other way around. He knew it all and then some. He had an understanding of Airbnb that no amount of access to privileged hosting data or first-hand hosting experience could teach. And he was eager to share.

We debated the merits of Airbnb hosting tactics over many more conversations. We were living parallel lives. We worked at companies we loved with exceptional co-workers but in jobs we hated. Rusteen was in accounting at Airbnb and I was in finance at an investment company. And we separately left the 9-5 grind in 2015 and began building our own Airbnb businesses that would eventually become LearnAirbnb.com and OptimizeMyAirbnb.com.

Rusteen's book is the culmination of not only his first-hand knowledge as a successful host, but also a unique combination of insider knowledge and his obsession to dissect the craft of hosting from multiple angles. Rusteen showcases how every choice you make as a host impacts your time, your profits, and your experience.

From the first step of preparing a unit and creating a listing to operational hacks that will save hosts hours, Airbnb hosts will find everything they need to start and run a successful Airbnb.

You don't know what you don't know. And these unknowns cost time, money, and unnecessary stress.

For all Airbnb hosts, *Optimize YOUR Airbnb* was written for you. Take notes.

Symon He
CEO, LearnAirbnb.com

Introduction

I started writing *Optimize YOUR Airbnb* in July 2017 while staying at an Airbnb in Estonia. I met Veronika while exploring Old Town Tallinn. When I found out Veronika was an Airbnb host, I asked to see her listing. I saw potential, but her online listing wasn't much. I told Veronika about how I optimize Airbnb listings. We agreed that I would stay at her listing at a small discount in exchange for a fully optimized Airbnb listing.

Veronika's ratings as of November 2017:

10 Reviews ★★★★★		Q Search reviews	
Accuracy	★★★★★	Location	★★★★★
Communication	★★★★★	Check In	★★★★★
Cleanliness	★★★★★	Value	★★★★★

I wrote *Optimize YOUR Airbnb* to reach more hosts like Veronika.
These pages contain the culmination of my five-year experience with Airbnb from being an employee and a guest, to a host, to Superhost, and to starting an Airbnb property management company

(belopm.com). I've hosted everything from a living room couch to a 3-story, 5-bedroom hillside mansion. The information in this book is more complete and effective than anything on the market. (I'd know. I read 13 of them.)

Prove it.

Here is a sliver of actionable tips right away (albeit easier to implement ones):

- ☐ Adding a ★ or ❤ to your title will increase your views.
- ☐ Adding your Uber referral code will earn you dozens of free rides.
- ☐ Adding a call-to-action in your text increases your conversion rate.

Special Features of This Book

My goal with this book is no different than my goal with your listing: to deliver as much information in the most efficient way. Please note some of the unique features you will find in this book:

1. Key points section at the beginning of each chapter
2. Bolded sentences of highly important points
3. Estimated reading time per chapter in the table of contents
4. 32 Pro Tips representing important, but tangentially related, points to the topic at hand
5. Visit OptimizeYourAirbnb.com to find links to recommended products and companies including discounts plus bonus content

'FPG' is used throughout the book and stands for 'Future Potential Guest'. An FPG represents a traveler with an upcoming trip to your location where your Airbnb listing is a potential option.

Who is this book for?

For the Airbnb host who wants an optimal online listing and off-line guest experience. And for the host with an open mind, many concepts I present run counter to what you've read prior. For example, I recommend only listing on one vacation rental platform, not taking photos of every angle of the room in favor of leaving something to the guest imagination, and not hiring a copywriter even if they specialize in vacation rentals. I don't go over basics like what a host profile is, instead I tell you how to properly create one to attract bookings based on a detailed study. I back up my strategies directly with Airbnb and third-party content.

Though this book was written with the Airbnb host in mind, the strategies can be applied to your platform of choice.

Don't choose budget for your Airbnb listing, and don't choose budget for your Airbnb knowledge.

About the Author

I'm Danny, The Airbnb Pro. In January 2013, a roommate introduced me to A-I-R-B-N-B during a conversation in my kitchen. Since then I have experienced Airbnb from every angle.

In April 2013, I booked my first guest trip on Airbnb to Santa Barbara, California.

> Daniel was a considerate guest and he left the house in good shape.
>
> April 2013
>
> Alex
> Kostruba

In July 2013, I started working at Airbnb in the finance department. In August 2013, I hosted my first guest on a couch in my living room.

Overview · Reviews · The Host · Location

CHEAP Comfy PERSONABLE Couch w ROOF DECK

Shared room in house · San Francisco
Hosted by Daniel Rusteen

👥 1 guest   🛏 1 bedroom   🛏 1 bed   🛁 1 bath

$45 per night
★★★★★ 87

Dates

Check In → Check Out

Guests

1 guest ⌄

In November 2014, I volunteered at the first Airbnb Open in San Francisco as an Airbnb employee.

In July 2015, I moved into the Local Operations department at Airbnb.

In October 2015, I became a Superhost. Here are my current stats:

Select date range		
Jan 1, 2017 – Dec 31, 2017 (Current)		⌄
	Superhost	You
Completed trips	10	20
Commitment rate	100%	100%
Response rate	90%	100%
5-star trips	80%	100%
Review rate	50%	100%

In November 2015, I attended the second Airbnb Open in Paris as a host.

In August 2016, I started an Airbnb property management company. All of my managed Airbnbs ranked on the first page of search.

Kentfield, CA						as of July 16, 2017 at 08:11
Dates	Your rate	Max	Min	Median	Average	Ranking
Jul 30 to Aug 6	$836	$2631	$282	$762	$995	1 /23
Jul 30 to Aug 7	$831	$2624	$278	$803	$1024	1 /22
Jul 30 to Aug 8	$828	$2618	$275	$780	$1033	1 /21
Jul 30 to Aug 9	$825	$2614	$273	$777	$1032	1 /21
Jul 30 to Aug 10	$823	$2610	$271	$774	$1030	1 /21
Jul 30 to Aug 11	$821	$2607	$270	$921	$1049	1 /20
Jul 30 to Aug 12	$819	$2605	$268	$919	$1049	1 /20
Jul 30 to Aug 13	$818	$10036	$267	$1012	$1523	1 /49
Jul 30 to Aug 14	$817	$10033	$298	$1034	$1650	1 /40
Jul 30 to Aug 15	$816	$10031	$297	$1067	$1706	1 /38
Jul 30 to Aug 16	$815	$10029	$296	$1071	$1706	1 /38
Jul 30 to Aug 17	$814	$10028	$296	$1111	$1760	1 /36

In November 2016, I attended the third Airbnb Open in Los Angeles as an Airbnb Property Manager.

In December 2016, I started OptimizeMyAirbnb.com. Here is the first version of that website as AnalyzeMyAirbnb.com:

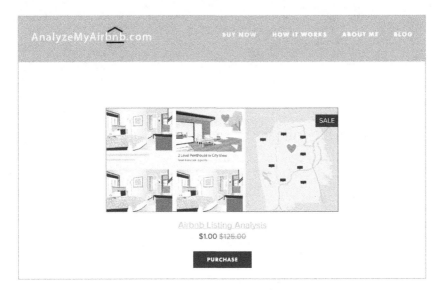

In July 2017, I became a digital nomad staying in Airbnbs around the world. Here is my current Airbnb profile:

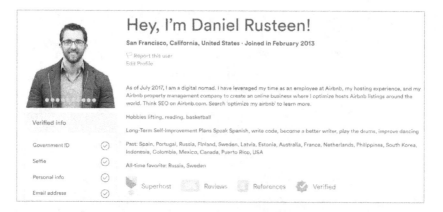

Here is one of my recent host reviews. When the host is open to improvement, I'm very forthcoming with advice:

Ali Alami Talbi

It was a great pleasure to host Danny. He is without a doubt a Five Star kind of guest, a seasoned world class traveler, a treasure of information. It is noteworthy to mention that Danny happens to also be a host with a remarkable hosting experience. I am so very greatful to Danny, he has gone far and beyond the extra mile in helping me with my listing and his advice and help was so valuable. He not only looked in every detail of my listings and was able to pinpoint all the weak spots but he also proceeded to show me how to better optimize every facet of my profile. I look forward to welcoming him back on his next visit to Casablanca.

Response from Daniel Rusteen:
WOW - This review brings a smile to my face. Glad you found my help so useful :D

Private Feedback:
Thanks Danny for all your help. We really appreciate it. Ali and I will come to visit one of these days in Cali. I am sure you will be a great host. Hope to see u soon. Take care. Omar and Ali.

November 2017

And, here is one recent guest review:

Maureen

Daniel's place was absolutely stunning located in a quiet neighborhood surrounded by beautiful redwood trees. The place was incredibly clean, comfortable, and spacious with amazing views. Daniel was an excellent host, very organized and responsive. My family and I had very positive and relaxing experience staying at Daniel's home. I would definitely recommend it to others, it's an unforgettable home.

From San Francisco, CA · September 2017 · ⚑ 🏠 2 Private Decks w 180° Views | Pool + Parking

The first listing I optimized was while I was an Airbnb property manager. I tweaked things within the listing and sometimes noticed a booking come in within hours. As I tweaked and added formulas to my process, results improved. That's when it hit me:

Google ranks websites based on a predictable set of variables. Airbnb must do the same thing.

I sold my first optimization report in June 2016. Since then, I've created more robust and personalized optimization reports for my hosts. To date, I've optimized over 500 Airbnb listings around the world from Sri Lanka to South Carolina.

Airbnb Explained
in 120 Words

Airbnb is not accommodations.

Or, hospitality.

Airbnb is connections.
Airbnb creates connections that never otherwise would have
existed, and they do this around the world every night.

Airbnb is trust.
The system works because guests are just as trusting *and nervous*
to spend the night in a stranger's home as hosts are to let them.

Airbnb singlehandedly is creating worldwide connections.
In an age of virtual experiences that distance people, Airbnb
encourages real, authentic, face-to-face experiences.

• • •

"I hope that's not the only thing you're working on," someone
said to Brian Chesky, Cofounder of Airbnb after he shared the
concept of his worldwide hosting company. But Chesky wasn't
looking at the world for what it was. Chesky was a visionary. Chesky
paved the way for a whole other way of looking at the world.

About Airbnb, an Insider's Perspective

In February 2013, I walked into the Airbnb offices at 99 Rhode Island, their third office since starting the company in August 2007, for an interview in the finance department. As soon as I walked into the office, I knew I made a mistake: working for a traditional company for three years before I found Airbnb. My first day at Airbnb was in July 2013. Two years later, I was fired. I walked out of the Airbnb headquarters wrapped up in a feeling of relief and started down a path that lead to this book.

Let's rewind to January 2013, when I heard about this company called A-I-R-B-N-B.

When I heard about Airbnb, I thought it was the greatest idea I had ever heard of. I looked them up. Light bulb. Airbnb was how I attempted to travel the world. I applied to Airbnb and got an interview. I didn't receive the job. Actually, no one was hired for the position I originally interviewed for. I remained in touch with Airbnb's recruiter. She told me four months later that another position had opened. As I walked through the doors for the second time, I was confident, but nervous. I knew deep down this was the single biggest moment of my entire life.

The employees were in jeans and shirts, shorts and sandals. Whizzing around on razor scooters, working in bean bag chairs, and smiling,

> • • •
>
> When I heard about Airbnb, I thought it was the greatest idea I had ever heard of. Airbnb was how I attempted to travel the world.
>
> • • •

I heard Airbnb employees ask each other, "Want another beer?" Calm and collected on the outside, my mind was bursting. For the first four months of my previous job, my office consisted of a non-adjustable chair at a picnic table shared with six accountants in a janitor's closet.

I was shocked a company office culture like Airbnb existed. Airbnb's culture was by design as I learned through the interview process. It was four days with 13 interviews including an off-site company happy hour. Every Friday, Airbnb employees would have a happy hour either at the office or in the city. The office was in the South of Market district in San Francisco and most employees lived there or in the nearby districts, so most offsite happy hours were in those neighborhoods. The happy hour I attended as part of my final interview was around the corner from my house in the northern most part of San Francisco. A 3-minute walk. The stars were aligned. This was my calling.

> • • •
>
> 'Don't fuck up the company culture.'
>
> • • •

I got the job. And a pay raise, stock options, a desk, adjustable chair, free food, yoga, and bike tune-ups. Life was good. I would start in July 2013 (Company Valuation: $2.5 Billion) in the new building at 888 Brannan Street.

Airbnb still occupies this space though when I moved in it was only on the 3rd floor. Then, the kitchen opened on the 5th floor. Then, the 4th floor opened with additional work space. Expansion was rapid. At one point, there were rumors of a gym, but Brian Chesky, Airbnb CEO and Co-founder and former body builder, confirmed he denied these plans in a company-wide meeting.

Company culture was artfully crafted by Chesky who often quotes Peter Thiel telling him 'Don't fuck up the company culture'[1]. Chesky took the advice to heart as evidenced by the founders being heavily involved in the interview process for the first five years of the company's growth.

The office was open. Zero employees, including the founders, had an office. Chesky's desk rotated between departments every few months. Looking back on it, the open office design provided an exciting company environment and culture, but low productivity. When the 4th floor

---

1   medium.com/@bchesky/dont-fuck-up-the-culture-597cde9ee9d4

opened, a new space called Belong Anywhere, the company slogan, was introduced where employees did not have an assigned desk. It didn't work for engineers or finance who needed an assigned desk, but it did for many other departments. You could reserve an Airbnb-inspired conference room. Breakfast, lunch, and dinner was initially served by the kitchen staff on the third floor in a makeshift dining room that doubled as office space and space for company wide meetings. A monthly email went out to schedule a free 15-minute massage and people frantically stopped whatever they were doing to sign up as there was limited space. Similar process when the free bike tune-ups email came around. It seemed like a quarter of the company rode their bikes to work.

• • •

All employees received $500 of Airbnb credit every quarter to use on these vacations.

• • •

Airbnb had holiday parties like I'd never seen before. I got to bring a date and opted to bring one of my good friends so I could finally show off my new company. Employees would dress up for Halloween and Christmas, often coordinating a team theme. Airbnb was a team. Every birthday was celebrated with all employees stopping what they were doing to share in cake. One of my first weeks in the office, the entire department took a full day off for team building activities. I loved every minute of it. It seemed like I didn't work more than a full day over the first month. But, this dissipated quickly.

My days were long from around 9am to 7pm. Some days I would stay until 8 or 9pm. My coworkers would get in as early as 6am. I learned this the day I showed up at 730am to get additional work done before a vacation and seeing three co-workers already at their desks typing away. We got 15 vacation days per year plus 10 days over Christmas, though, this was supposed to be a surprise and the powers that be would deliver the good news so late the prices for flights were sky high. Nevertheless, we were all still extremely grateful. All employees received $500 of Airbnb credit every quarter to use on these vacations.

I remember ordering packages to the office mail room and having to spell out A-I-R-B-N-B when ordering by phone. Airbnb still sounded like gibberish to most people in 2014 (Company Valuation: $10 Billion). Despite our growth rate and valuation, the unaided awareness in 2014 in the US was only at 6%.

Proposition F, a ballot measure to limit Airbnb in San Francisco, in late 2014 (Company Valuation: $13 Billion) helped to get the word out on Airbnb, at least locally, as many people even in San Francisco hadn't even heard Airbnb. As Chesky said, Airbnb was a perfect target as we were in the middle of the tech scene (gentrification, tech bros, big busses driving through the small San Francisco streets to take employees to the Google offices down south) and real estate (tenants rights activists, sky high rents, and evictions). At one point, a protest made its way into the Airbnb HQ and employees looked down as people let up balloons with words blaming Airbnb for the city's housing crisis. They didn't know any better.

> • • •
> Airbnb was a perfect target as we were in the middle of the tech scene and real estate, both hot button issues in San Francisco.
> • • •

Two traditions actually strengthened as the company grew: food and company-wide meetings including happy hours. The food was always good, but kept getting better. The kitchen staff, full-time Airbnb employees, always outdid themselves with meals, desserts, and celebrations. We celebrated Thanksgiving at the office, Mother's Day, and any other statutory holiday.

Airbnb did an outstanding job of communicating to their employees what was going on at the company. On Tuesday mornings, we would have global company meetings which would update everyone on recent developments and features. On Friday, it would be just for the HQ and would end in a happy hour. Once a month, we would do Formal Friday where everyone would dress up in proper business clothes. Chesky would often lead these meetings. He was an entertaining public speaker. I learned about his body building days and the infamous 'pocket steak' story in which he used to work as a movie theatre security guard and carried a cooked steak in a plastic bag in his pant pocket as he had to eat a serving of protein every few hours during these meetings. It's here also that I would learn of non-accounting terminology like P1, P2, and P3 – the different pages on the Airbnb website. P1 is the home page. P2 is the search results. P3 is the listing page where you could book. You could always book a listing within three clicks which was inspired by the late Steve Jobs, one of Chesky's idols, mimicking the amount of clicks before you could play a song on the iPod.

I loved the company and the team around me, but accounting just wasn't something I ever remotely loved doing. I was never cut out to be an accountant. I would get in trouble for not being in my desk enough. I would socialize as I got so much more enjoyment from that aspect of my job. I justified it by telling myself that the more I socialized, I was giving a face to the accounting department in the company. Unlike other companies I had been a part of, the accounting department seemed well respected at Airbnb. There were a lot of heavy hitters, a lot of really smart people on that team. I probably did not take advantage of my surrounding intellectual power enough.

Whenever anything else came up work related, but not accounting related, I would volunteer. Airbnb hosted fireside chats with famous people. The most famous were Joe Montana and Marissa Mayor. I attended almost all the fireside chats.

I started a Toastmasters club which would give me an excuse to do something else and leave work early one day a week to facilitate meetings or give speeches. I would routinely respond to emails asking for employee hosts to help with testing new features and experiments. At the first Airbnb Open in San Francisco in 2014, I volunteered my entire weekend there.

• • •

Whenever anything else came up work related, but not accounting related, I would volunteer. .

• • •

Internally, there was One Airbnb in which all employees were flown to headquarters in San Francisco for a week to meet each other. We were supposed to get work done this week, but I would do the bare minimum, opting to socialize instead. Airbnb had a basketball team. I joined. Joe Gebbia was also on the team. He's pretty good at basketball. Quick with a good shot and solid defense.

Around April 2015, (Company Valuation: $25.5 Billion) during a Friday meeting, a new employee in Local Operations, Brian Martinez, announced a program that would pay employees $500 for every host referral they brought in. At the time, I didn't think much of it until I had a brief chat with Martinez who said the winner would be announced and awarded a prize. This was the real incentive for me. I was always looking for ways to be on stage and announced to the company as I knew it wouldn't come from my accounting work. Over the next few weeks, I leveraged my contacts, created marketing material, and brought in 36 referrals.

Then, I was fired. It wasn't a good fit, professionally. Over the course of a few months and serious conversations I knew my time was coming to an end at Airbnb unless I could do something drastic. I tried to change departments. After some in-depth research into the different departments and sub-departments in Airbnb, I decided the only one I wanted to join was the Business Travel team in the Business Development department. I made my case as persuasively as I could, but at the end of the day, the decision makers couldn't wrap their head around an accountant being good as a business developer. I went on to business develop a local Airbnb property management company to triple their revenues the next year.

> . . .
> I was on the right bus, but in the wrong seat the whole time.
> . . .

Anyways, a mentor in finance I deeply respect advised me that it's not fair to Airbnb or me having me do accounting. My skills are better suited elsewhere. It was a tough goodbye because I loved Airbnb. At the same time, I felt oddly relieved. It felt like a huge weight was lifted off my shoulders. I no longer have to do accounting. Now, I can find what I really want to do in life. Plus, walking away with $15,000 in Airbnb credit due to the promotion eased the pain.

Second place finished with twelve referrals. Because of this and thanks to Brian Martinez, I was re-hired a week later as a contractor in a similar role. Due to my performance with the promotion, I didn't even have to interview. I was now a Host Ambassador. All the folks I told I was leaving kept seeing me around and they got very confused. I loved it. I flourished in this new role. I was on the right bus, but in the wrong seat the whole time. Over the next six months, I would beat out everyone on the new team signing up the most new hosts, getting the highest conversion rate, and booking the most reservations.

I officially said goodbye to Airbnb in January 2016 (Company Valuation: $30 Billion) as my contractor role dried up under the intense political pressure put on Airbnb by San Francisco. The city the company was founded in hated them. Local tenant's rights groups blamed Airbnb for evictions and ever-increasing rent. Hotel lobbies funded any opposition to Airbnb that made them appear as dangerous tax-avoiding rebels. They didn't know any better.

PART I

Your Online Airbnb Listing

> "I didn't have time to write a short letter, so I wrote a long one instead."
> – *Mark Twain*

CHAPTER 1

Snappy, Catchy, + Thorough: Your Airbnb Listings Mantra

Key Points

▶ Give FPGs the most information in the most digestible way possible.

▶ Provide information to the guest only when it's useful to them.

▶ Your listing's cover photos have the sole purpose of attracting eyes and clicks.

▶ Communicate positive and negative aspects of your listing to help with 5-star reviews by setting expectations before the guest checks-in.

To attract and keep an FPGs attention is an art, an art that requires you to give them the most information in the least amount of words. Sounds simple enough, but it is not (refer to above quote). Time and again, I see hosts load up their listing's page to the brim with behemoth descriptions. These descriptions come in run-on sentences and as blocks of text that are not pleasing to the eye.

Tangent: Keep in mind there are many points in the reservation process. Certain information is best communicated at certain points in that process. Do not overload the guest with irrelevant information.

As a society, our collective attention span has decreased to at most, a few minutes, and at least to how quickly one can flick their finger across a mobile screen thanks to Snapchat, Instagram, and Tinder. In fact, the average web browser stays on a webpage for between ten and twenty seconds. Let's assume this is true for Airbnb. Furthermore, there is intense competition on Airbnb.

How will you stand out, knowing there are tens, possibly hundreds, of listings like yours? You should make your listing snappy, catchy, and thorough. This should be at the back of your mind throughout the entire Airbnb listing creation process:

- Catchy to grab attention
- Snappy to keep attention
- Thorough to attract the right guest

Here are a few examples (remember, snappy, catchy, and thorough applies to your entire listing):

Cover photo

The cover photo needs to feature a selling point of your listing. The cover photo's sole purpose is to attract eyes and clicks. Scout the competition in your area and find out which colors are not being used in their cover photos and plan accordingly. You will want it to be a photo of a room your guest will be spending a lot of time in including a bedroom, a living room, or the kitchen. Rarely should a listing's cover photo be a view. A view will probably be similar for listings in the area and should left to delight the guest upon arrival.

Title

Communicate a selling point to your guest, ideally an amenity not typically available in your area. Be catchy. Do not tell the guest how many bedrooms your listing has. They have probably already narrowed down the search result if they are serious about booking.

- Bad title: 2 bed/1 bath elegant spacious home in Sunset District
- Good title: Rooftop Patio w Views/Hot Tub + Parking

Description

Keep your description snappy, yet thorough. It is best to communicate the good and bad aspects of your listing in your description. A guest surprised by 27 steps leading into your listing could lead to a bad review. Set expectations of your guest prior to booking.

- Bad: My spacious home has all the details of a traditional Victorian in the heart of San Francisco's Hayes Valley. When you arrive, you'll experience a San Franciscan stair case so pack your walking shoes!
- Good (using a bullet point): 27 steps into my home from street level.

Always consider the cost of disclosing information. For example, it's cool that you splurged on 2,000 thread count Egyptian cotton for your bed linens. The guests may appreciate the linens, but they will not book your listing because of them. Leave it out of your description. It will be a "surprise and delight" feature, something the guest will happily discover upon check-in.

Keep in mind the guests will receive a House Manual from Airbnb upon confirmation. Do not overload the guest with pages of information here. The House Manual should only contain the most important house rules the guest needs to know at time of booking. All else should be delivered with your electronic House Manual four days before check-in. Refer to Chapter 18: Optimizing and Automating Your Messages for details on message format and timing.

> "To say that great photos of your space are valuable is an understatement. They're the first thing prospective guests look at when considering a property on Airbnb and what will eventually make or break their decision to book your space."
>
> *– Airbnb[2]*

Use Your Phone to Take Better Photos

Key Points

- ▶ Part of taking great photos is staging the room.
- ▶ Using a camera app, shoot multiple angles of each room. Choose the best later.
- ▶ HDR, high dynamic range, is your best friend.
- ▶ Consider your lighting – for outdoor photos, the sun should always be behind you.
- ▶ Using an editing app like Snapseed, apply minor editing where needed.
- ▶ Optional: a tripod, microfiber cloth, and wide-angle lens phone attachment.

We wholeheartedly agree with the quote above. But in our experience, that has not translated into universally attractive listing photos.

No judgment. We get it. No one stumbles into being a lawyer or a dentist. But many Airbnb hosts got into the business without background training or education in sales, marketing, interior design,

AUTHOR'S NOTE: This chapter was written by Kati and Brian from Overlooked2Overbooked.com, where they teach you how to take the best photos possible while using your camera phone and basic editing.

---

2   blog.atairbnb.com/top-5-photo-tips-for-a-stellar-listing/

photography, or any of the other myriad skills necessary to run a successful VR business.

The good news is producing great photos for your listing isn't as hard as you might think, but it does require a bit of effort and some planning.

This chapter will unleash the full potential of your camera phone and your photography abilities. We will explain how to stage your listing, how to use the most important camera settings on your phone, and how to edit these photos.

How to Clean and Stage

You must present your space in the best possible light (pun intended). No, you are not deceiving the guest by making the space look its best any more than you're deceiving the dentist by flossing just before your appointment. The goal is to get your space looking great all the time, so start with prepping for your photo shoot.

Decorating doesn't have to be expensive. If you're short on art, flower vases, or decorative bowls, visit a thrift store. Used books, magazines, and games are a perfect way to fill in a book case and give your guests some entertainment. Every room is staged differently and there are key points to remember for each.

> • • •
>
> "If bad decorating was a hanging offense, there'd be bodies hanging from every tree."
>
> —*Sylvester Stallone*
>
> • • •

Kitchens & Bathrooms

- Pay attention to shiny surfaces because water stains can jump out in photos.
- Display only essentials in a bathroom, like hand soap and rolled up towels.
- Close the toilet seat.
- In the kitchen, organize loose items, like spices or tea and coffee containers.
- Remove dishes, dish racks, and sponges.

- Show off attractive amenities, but don't leave countertops looking cluttered.
- Set up a bowl of fruit or flowers on a table, or a bottle of wine with some glasses.

Living Area

- Take any pillows or blankets and stage your couch and chairs for comfort as if to invite guests to rest there.
- Turn on a fireplace if you've got it.
- Lay a book on the coffee table.
- Keep the TV off, it's hard to make it look good for a photo while on.
- Hide any wires (Recommended product on book website).
- Make sure windows are clean.
- If you have a balcony or a terrace, open the doors.

Bedrooms

- Clean windows and straighten curtains.
- Minimize bedding wrinkles by pulling on each corner instead of smoothing them out with your hand.
- Stack pillows in layers.
- Stage a few rolled up towels, maybe with a soap, at the foot of the bed.
- Open doors to a balcony.

Balcony/ Terrace / Pool

This is the place to wow guests and emphasize relaxation.

- Make your amenities and outdoor spaces look presentable and inviting.
- Brush off leaves, grab a book, a towel, and a drink to stage a sun chair by the pool.
- Add a couple cushions to deck stairs and showcase a clean bar-beque, if you have it.

How to Become a Whiz with your Camera (in less than an hour)

The most important tool for taking great photos is the photographer. The person using the camera should know enough about it so it is insignificant what kind of camera they are using.

First, download one of the following camera phone apps:

Camera+ (iPhone)   Open Camera (android)

These will help you start with the best possible base and minimize editing as you'll be starting with proper functionality. If not already on, turn on a grid with two vertical and two horizontal lines.

Exposure and Focus

It's important that you know how to control the exposure (brightness) of your photos and that your photos are sharp and in focus. On many phones, the most basic way to adjust exposure and focus is to click on the screen of the device and a little icon appears. This tells the camera "I want this part to be bright and in focus" and the camera will adjust accordingly.

White Balance

White balance is the camera's ability to present colors in the photo as they appear in real life. Generally, the auto white balance (AWB) function in most cameras is good enough to automatically evaluate the image and not make it too blue or yellow. But if something goes haywire, find your White Balance setting and check if your preset is wrong. In the settings, you'll often find presets like 'a sunny day', 'an overcast day', and some options for adjusting to indoor lamps. These adjustments can be quite drastic, so the safest bet is to stay in auto mode. Any change you make from AWB shows up immediately on the screen.

Lock Your Look

When shooting in auto mode, the camera adjusts for exposure, focus, and white balance every time you move the camera. Sometimes, you'll want to override those settings and lock in what you think looks good.

In devices without specialty camera settings, you can do this by tapping and holding on the screen. An icon should appear that tells the exposure and focus you chose are now 'locked in'. You may also see a little lock icon. Now when you move the camera, it won't constantly re-adjust.

HDR: stands for High Dynamic Range

HDR is your best friend. It is a setting with which you combine multiple exposures, from dark to bright, and merge them into one image. This way, you get to keep the details visible in both the highlights and the shadows of your image. Ever see a photo where you can't see what's outside of the window, but the actual room looks great? HDR attempts to fix that so you can see the view.

Phones and photo apps come with an HDR mode, so if you have it, by all means use it. This helps bring down things like bright windows, while "lifting" the shadows, like a dark room.

How to Execute a Successful Vacation Rental Photo Shoot

The number one thing that creates pleasant photos and minimizes the time you have to spend editing them is working with available light. **Don't shoot against the sun. Use the sun as a light source by keeping it behind you.**

This tip is especially helpful outdoors. This way, the sun will help light the subject for you instead of beaming straight into the lens creating harsh contrasts and a hazy image.

When indoors, avoid aiming straight at windows when bright sunlight is coming in. Camera lenses can't handle the contrast between bright windows and a dark room.

Our favorite kinds of days for shooting interiors are partly cloudy days. The clouds help mute the sunlight and make views through windows easier to capture while still creating bright rooms.

When you begin taking photos inside, **turn on all the lights and open doors.** Open the curtains, and maybe a window where appropriate. Open doors not only let in more light and help connect spaces, but they also create an inviting atmosphere.

Wipe your camera lens with a microfiber cloth. Any that you use on your glasses will work. You'd be surprised how much we touch the lens accidentally and even a little bit of dirt or grease from fingers can wreak havoc on photo quality.

The three biggest mistakes people make when taking photos are:

1. **They step too far into the room.**
2. **Lift the camera to eye level.**
3. **Point the camera down at furniture.**

These errors result in cropped photos that make rooms look small and uninviting.

Instead:

1. **Step back as far as possible in a given room, maybe even outside the room, until something like a door frame comes in view.**
2. **Lower the camera to about waist level.**
3. **Point straight ahead into the room, not down.**

These three steps make rooms appear larger and give guests a better idea of what a space looks like. These steps also keep vertical lines in the photo straight (vertical lines converging make a room look small).

Another way to add depth and character to a room is to **aim your camera at the corners of the room.** As you tuck into one corner of the room, aim for the opposite corner. Remember to keep your camera low. So low in fact, that you may want to kneel down to get a better view. But not so low that you can see under cabinets or tables.

If something, like a kitchen island is blocking your view try to find a better angle. And if that doesn't work, lift the camera a little and point it slightly downwards. We'll straighten those converging lines later. Pull lighter items, like chairs, out of the way when necessary.

Take a photo from every angle in a given room to have more options later. Keep in mind the best angle of a room might not be where you enter.

In the kitchen, capture an angle that's facing the stove top and major appliances. The more you can include in one shot, the better. Beware of your own reflection off of appliances.

In bedrooms, always get an angle from one corner of the (foot of) the bed, aiming diagonally at the opposite (headboard) corner. Stand back as far back as possible. Try to include something interesting in any area without a bed, like a balcony, door, cabinet, or artwork.

In bathrooms, **you can ignore the toilet.** It should not be the focus of any bathroom photo. If you cannot get all major elements into one shot, try to aim for the sink and mirror combo You don't have to show everything.

PRO TIP: You may consider a wide-angle lens here which increases the camera's field of view. I recommend this one: www.amzn.to/2hyP5wB.

In living areas, don't be afraid to get into awkward spaces for the best view and widest angle. Avoid showing just the backs of sofas, which means you may have to lift and slightly point the camera down.

For outdoor shots, aiming at a corner is a good idea, as this adds depth to the house and makes it feel grand. Capture several things at once, the yard, pool, and deck, by venturing out to the backyard.

Take your photos at a time of day when the sun illuminates the house (i.e. it's behind you). Avoid photographing your house when it's in a shadow (shadows are the enemy), or aiming your camera straight into the sun. **A great time of day for exteriors is Golden Hour. This is the time just after sunrise and just before sunset, when the sun is low and the light is warm.**

How to Edit Your Photos

First, backup all originals. Use a cloud service, like Google Drive or Microsoft's One Drive (Outlook and Hotmail), or a hard drive for uploading photos.

Adjustments

With any editing software, the basic adjustments are:

Crop – To make the photo smaller in some way, in case you want to remove something in the original photo.

Exposure / brightness – For making your photo brighter or darker.

Rotate – For slightly rotating the photo to keep horizons straight.

Saturation – For making colors pop.

Advanced adjustments to look for:

Highlights – For bringing down the brightest parts of a photo, like clouds.

Perspective / Vertical Distortion / Lens Corrections – For straightening vertical lines.

Shadows – For bringing up the darkest parts of a photo.

The majority of phone photo editing apps allow for those basic adjustments, as well as Highlight and Shadow controls. Our favorite is Snapseed.

As you bring, or 'import' photos into your editing tool, turn off Auto Brightness on your device and bring the screen brightness to the max.

> **PRO TIP:** Take your photo editing to the next level by editing on your computer with Adobe Lightroom (lightroom.adobe.com). You can sign up for a free trial through the link.

Selections

Before you get into editing, make a first round of selection. Pick the best photo of the photos you've shot. If you cannot decide between angles, choose too many rather than too few for now. After editing, you can always cut photos from the group before you upload them to a listing.

We recommend having 20 photos, if possible. If you have a studio apartment, this will be hard to do so you can include some photos of your neighborhood and street. Don't push for 20 as you don't want to lose the FPGs attention. The minimum is 12.

Editing

The most important thing is to constantly evaluate your image and know when you've gone too far. Ideally with editing, we're trying to capture the feel of a place and attempt to match the human eye.

The second most important thing to do, is find how you undo a setting. In many tools, you'll find a back arrow or an X that indicate undoing a setting.

Exposure

Adjust your exposure, sometimes simply called brightness, so your photo is nice and bright. Your subject, be it the inside of a room or artwork, should be clearly visible. Don't make a room dark just to show a sliver of a view through a window.

Highlights and Shadows

Often changing your exposure will make the highlights, meaning the brightest parts of the photo, too bright. Bright windows and clouds tend to turn into big, bright blobs of light. Next, find the highlights adjustment and bring them down. Not so far that they look grey, but just a little bit.

Then, if your shadows, meaning the darkest parts of the photo, are only barely visible, find the shadow adjustment, and bring them out. Again, not so far that the image has no natural shadows. Just up enough where the shadows are no longer incomprehensibly dark.

Saturation

Saturation affects the intensity of colors. Most photos could benefit from a little saturation, especially outdoors. You really want the blue of the sky or an ocean and green grass to pop. When you add saturation, keep an eye out for red colors. Those tend to quickly turn into big red blobs.

Straighten and Crop

After the basic adjustments, make sure your photos are straight. Straight horizontal and vertical lines are more aesthetically pleasing in photos. Often the adjustments for straightening a photo are under a setting called crop. The majority of editing tools will have a way to rotate a photo. This is great for making sure your horizon is straight, which is especially important when you have a clean horizontal line, like the line between an ocean and the sky.

Indoors is when vertical lines become the focal point. Some editing apps will allow you to adjust these too. Look for a tool that's like a distorted square that's called something like perspective or straighten. Keep an eye on the major vertical lines, like walls, doorways, and windows.

Perspective

Find a vertical line at the center of the image and rotate the image until that line is straight. This is where a grid will be very helpful. Then, keep an eye on the major vertical lines near the edges, like walls, doorways, and windows, and use the Perspective tool until those lines are straight as well. Visit Overbooked2Overlooked.com for a thorough explanation with photo examples.

Exporting

Export or save your photos in their original, largest size because listing platforms prefer these higher-quality images.

Then, backup your edited, final photos to a cloud service or hard drive.

Authors' Conclusion

Your photos are well into the top 20% of all vacation rental property photos.

Brian and Kati offer a more detailed, three-part video series on their website at Overlooked2Overbooked.com. I have taken the course and was blown away that using a camera phone while knowing which settings to turn on with light editing can produce top quality photos.

CHAPTER 3

5 Photo Tips for More Reservations

Key Points

▶ Bright, professional photos are a must.
▶ Review photos during the shoot to avoid re-shoots.
▶ Choose your cover photo based on your competitions cover photo. If they all show a backyard pool, show something else.
▶ The first five to seven cover photos matter most, ensure these are varied and are the absolute best!
▶ Batch your photos to create a virtual tour. Especially important for larger homes.
▶ More than 30 photos is overboard for 90%+ of Airbnb listings.

Photos are as important to Airbnb listings as marshmallows and chocolate are to s'mores—without that gooey, attractive, melty filling, who will want to take a bite? If you want to influence FPGs to book your listing, photos are the most important first impression you can establish. Said differently: They are very, very important! I have assembled a list of the top five tips for having successful photos to represent your beautiful Airbnb listing.

Ever Seen a Superhost with Mediocre Photos?

Before you even have your listing up, you should either sign up for professional photography from Airbnb[3] or hire a local residential,

---

3   www.airbnb.com/info/photography

interior photographer. Be sure not to active your listing. As a new host, you get an automatic boost in rankings for the first 30 days after you put your listing up. However, if you get a lot of views and no reservations during this time, Airbnb deems your listing as low quality, and your listing goes to the end of the search results. You need to capitalize on that initial boost by having great photos that encourage FPGs to click on your listing.

Keep in mind, **not all photographers are made equal.** This is especially important when it comes to Airbnb photographers: it is a one-time, paid service with no revisions, so you need to capitalize on it. Now, while 90% of my own encounters have been with wonderful, creative, and experienced photographers, occasionally there are some who miss the mark. **Ask to see the photos during the shoot: it is better to find out now if you will be unhappy.** Twenty pictures emphasizing your ceiling over your appliances, furniture, and ambiance of your home will not leave a good impression, and you will end up having to hire a new photographer to try again.

Note: If you go with an Airbnb photographer, the old photos will remain in your listing once the new ones are uploaded. You need to delete the old photos and rearrange the new photos as I will discuss below.

Do Judge A Listing By Its Cover

Now that you understand the importance of photos to your listing, can you guess which photo is the most important? The first, or cover, photo is your invaluable first impression. The cover photo should be of a room that the guest is likely to spend a lot of their time in or one that best represents the spirit of your home. Do you have an amazing living space or a luxurious bathroom? Does your futuristic kitchen scream, "Let's have a dinner party?" Avoid photos that encourage suspicions, such as nondescript views from a balcony or dimly lit backyards, and put your best photo forward. Get your FPG excited to see what your listing has to offer.

Before a guest clicks on any listing, they will have seen at least a few other cover photos. Make yours a great one.

PRO TIP: Go on Airbnb as if you are a FPG and do a few varied searches to find out what cover photos your competition is using. Are there any consistent colors? Themes? Rooms? For example:

Clearly, there are more than a few backyard pools in Seminyak, Bali. This means having a pool is not a unique selling point, so consider how to make your cover photo stand out. Hot tub, anyone?

Here is an example of what not to do with your cover photo. The host is wasting nearly 50% of their cover photo real estate:

Airbnb has stated that a horizontal photo will directly increase a listings rank in search[4].

---

4   blog.atairbnb.com/search

First (Five) Impressions Matter

Now that you have chosen an extraordinary cover photo, pay special attention to your main five photos. These are your best photos, one of each room, shown to your guest to get them excited about booking your place. **The FPG will decide within the first five to seven seconds to either eliminate your listing or keep it in the running, based on the cover and your first four photos.** There are over 3,000,000 listings on Airbnb[5], and guests will look for any reason to narrow their choices.

Batch 'Em

Keep in mind that the FPG will be looking at many listings with different layouts, and they have never been to your listing before. Even though you may look at your new photos and clearly picture your home, an FPG may get confused by similar rooms or different angles. Take your prospective guest on an organized, guided tour of your home by placing photos of the same room or space next to each other.

Take a look at the photos below:

---

5   www.airbnb.com/about/about-us

These photos came to me from a host seeking help optimizing his listing. Would you believe me if I told you these are four different bedrooms? Look closely. This host originally had 79 photos in random order, making it very difficult for the guest to know what they were looking at. In the end, this host was left with 34 orderly, batched photos, where the guest could easily know what they were looking at. As we'll see in the next section, captions helped here, too (as did a floor plan).

> **PRO TIP:** **More than 30 photos is overkill for 90%+ of Airbnb listings. Stick to around 25 photos maximum.** If you have a one-story home with few separate rooms, consider 10-15 photos and add a few of the neighborhood. Less is more!

The Power of Captions

Most pictures should have a caption, which will accomplish two goals.

- **One, the caption will explain to the guest where they are within the home, and create a physical sense of space.** Similar to our "Batch 'Em" principle, always assume that a FPG does not know what they are looking at, no matter how obvious it may be to you. Tell your guest about the decadent private bathroom attached to the master bedroom, or the French sliding doors that lead to your backyard garden. In other words, call out a unique feature of the photo (probably something in the background) that the guest may miss with a quick glance. Label bedrooms and bathrooms to provide clarity. Instead of having one wide-angle photo of the entire room then a close up of the closet, nightstand, and desk, call out any special items in the caption. The caption should be used to draw attention to the photo, especially if the guest is likely to miss a certain feature.

- **Two, place the guest, psychologically, in each photo, and in the listing.** This is a twist on one of Robert Cialdini's six principles of persuasion, commitment, and consistency[6]. Humans want to be consistent with their behavior, so if you place

---

6 *Influence: The Psychology of Persuasion by Robert Cialdini* (amzn.to/2sUgg9s)

the guest psychologically in your listing, their brain will start to think that they are already in your listing. It is a small mind trick, and the reason many actors take on the personas of their on-screen characters in real life. For example, picture a photo of your backyard with a pool and lounge chairs captioned, "Imagine yourself relaxing on the lounge chair, glass of wine in hand, surrounded by family and good conversation."

PRO TIP: **Keep your captions to one line. Otherwise, you risk having it overlap your actual photo, which is not aesthetically pleasing.**

3/49: Comes perhaps for this place. A view to Lenangstindene (Store Lenangstinden, 1625 m) from

Great Photos = More Bookings

In summary, optimizing your photos with free professional photography, a great cover photo, batched photos, first impression photos, and captions is a first step in attracting more FPGs to click and book your listing.

CHAPTER 4

Mastering the Title

Key Points

▶ Your Airbnb title may be cut off on mobile devices so focus on the first half.

▶ Use a symbol to attract more eyeballs and clicks.

▶ Make it 50 characters as Airbnb search favors longer titles.

▶ Do not use any adjectives.

▶ Include top amenities in your title.

▶ Do not use CAPITAL LETTERS.

▶ Typically, do not mention your neighborhood.

The Airbnb title is for your guest not you. Excluding price and location which are filtered prior to any titles being read, your title is the second most important feature of your Airbnb listing, behind the almighty cover photo. My guess is **90%+ of Airbnb hosts are not getting their title right.** Given how many hosts overvalue their property in terms of their nightly rate, it is surprising to see so many lackluster titles:

Beautiful, Relaxing Home Near Downtown

Private, Quiet, Comfy, Clean Room

Two Bedroom Condo in Amazing Location

By the end of this chapter, you will understand what should go into (and stay out of) your Airbnb title.

Focus on the front of your Airbnb title

May I demonstrate?

$59 ⚡⚡ Quiet Comfortable Room Overlo...
Private room
★★★★★ 104 Reviews

$61 ⚡⚡ Cozy, Private Studio Flat 21 mi...
Entire guesthouse
★★★★★ 190 Reviews

Ouch!

21...miles from what? Seems far.

Over...overlooking a dump?

Maybe I am overreacting. It is 'Overlooking Garden' and '21 minutes from downtown', but hopefully you can see the point. **On mobile phones or tablets and sometimes desktops, the end of an Airbnb title may be cut off.**

Using symbols in your Airbnb title

Using symbols in Airbnb titles is my most powerful technique. I use a range of symbols for listings I optimize. In the past, I have used music notes, arrows, sunrises, chess pieces, wingdings, check marks, figures, numbers, happy faces, and degree symbols. But, the most common ones I use are the star (☆) or the heart (♥). Instead of saying 'heart of downtown', use the symbol to communicate the same information in fewer characters. Do not overdo it, though. Use three symbols maximum.

Your Airbnb title should be 50 characters or damn close

Airbnb favors listings with longer titles. The maximum length of any title is 50 words so get to it or within a few characters of it. Refer to Figure 10 of this Airbnb search analysis[7].

Page #	# of listings	Price/Bed	Name Length	% of InstantBook	Reviews	Times Saved to Wishlist
1	109	$ 56.43	5.4	62.4%	13.17	143.6
2	111	$ 62.85	5.3	39.6%	11.58	122.5
3	106	$ 69.90	5.3	35.8%	7.79	95.4
4	104	$ 73.15	5.0	34.6%	6.05	76.5
5	101	$ 76.08	5.4	34.7%	6.18	56.8
6	104	$ 75.60	4.9	26.9%	3.34	47.0
7	109	$ 95.39	5.1	24.8%	3.65	43.3
8	95	$ 94.27	4.9	22.1%	3.23	36.8
9	99	$ 84.93	5.0	21.2%	2.73	33.6
10	93	$ 75.12	5.0	24.7%	2.53	41.5
11	92	$ 117.15	4.9	17.4%	3.57	43.6
12	101	$ 89.00	4.5	18.8%	1.55	32.4
13	105	$ 87.77	4.8	22.9%	2.41	41.9
14	96	$ 107.85	4.4	19.8%	1.93	26.7
15	84	$ 135.16	4.7	11.9%	2.89	40.4
16	86	$ 112.68	4.7	7.0%	1.90	28.1
17	43	$ 130.16	4.1	20.9%	1.81	24.9
Grand Total	1638	$ 88.52	5.0	27.1%	4.74	57.7

Figure 10: Factors 6-10 correlating to higher search ranks

Avoid generic adjectives in your Airbnb title

Do not use adjectives in your Airbnb title. If you have any of the following words in your title, immediately change them:

- Cozy
- Comfy
- Convenient
- Central
- Charming
- Renovated
- Luxury
- Studio, Condo, Townhouse, apartment, home, house, etc.

---

7   goo.gl/tSggs1

You do not want to use these because **they are generic and do not communicate any useful information to the FPG** who is looking at a dozen other listings. You need to grab their attention; Your Airbnb depends on it. Telling them your home is quiet and convenient and in a central location is not going to accomplish that objective.

I want to comment on 'luxury' and 'renovated' which are tier two adjectives. These adjectives at least provide a bit more context, but you still do not want to use them in your title:

- Luxury – The photos will communicate luxury to the guest. **You want to communicate as much information to the guest in the least amount of time** so this becomes an unneeded word. Delete it. Plus, if your home truly is luxurious, you will likely need to describe what makes it so, for example 'heated bathroom floors.'

- Renovated – The pictures will also communicate this, but you need to add what was renovated and when. This is great to include in the 'About this listing' section, for example, 'completely renovated in 2017' tells a guest, they will not have any hot water, heating, electricity, or Wi-Fi issues.

Do not use the Airbnb title to identify one of your listings

I am looking at you, property managers. More than once I have seen generic codes in listings. It is always a property manager trying to identify the listing for themselves while totally disregarding the FPG. I get it, makes life easier for you. But, it does not make life easier for the FPG. Well, it sort of does. It makes their life easier by easily looking over your listing in favor of one with a better title.

Montbleu Suites 1 @ Lost World of Tambun

Ulu Kinta, Perak, Malaysia ★★★★☆ 20 reviews

Montbleu Suites

Airbnb has rolled out a feature to some hosts where you can give an internal name to your listing that only you see. It can be found in the title section when in edit mode:

Title and description

Add a title and description to help guests get an idea of what it'll be like to stay in your place.

Internal name
only you'll see this

Tropical Paradise #1

English

Title
Enter your English listing name.

Secluded Tropical Garden Near Beach

Use your amenities to sell the guest

Do you live in a city with a lot of parking issues, but have a parking space for the guest? Do you have a private rooftop with a hot tub overlooking Sydney Harbor? How about a back patio with a fire pit?

Then let the guest know in the Airbnb title. Other less dazzling, but still unique and useful amenities are:

- Fireplace
- Washer + dryer
- HBO or Netflix
- Garden

Under the right circumstances, these may all be used in your Airbnb title.

CAPITAL LETTERS

To me, capital letters seem to be connected with low quality and 'scammy' behavior. The obvious point is to stick out and draw more attention to your listing. Capital letters expands the space needed for each character on the screen which allows you less visible words, especially on mobile devices. **I do not use capitals for my listings or the listings I optimize.**

Do not add your neighborhood

Not adding your neighborhood in your title is a controversial recommendation. I know people who recommend using the neighborhood especially a well-known one. I rarely use neighborhood names in titles. I assume one of two things:

1. The FPG does not know anything about your specific neighborhood so telling them is not going to encourage them to book. Save the words for something that is.
2. Either the neighborhood is so popular that the FPG already knows about it or they have done their research and narrowed the Airbnb search map based on the neighborhood area they want to stay in.

One exception might be if two drastically different neighborhoods are bordering each other. Let's say one is known for crime and the other is upscale and your home is on the border. These neighborhoods do exist, for example Nob Hill and Tenderloin neighborhoods in San Francisco. Some people refer unofficially to the whole area as Tender-Nob. In this case, I may specify in the title or somewhere prominent that my listing is in the upscale neighborhood.

Piedmont is a small, residential, upper-class neighborhood that no one's ever heard of while Oakland is generically known for crime. Most guests coming to the area do not know the nitty-gritty on what parts of Oakland are good or bad, so it *might* make sense to call out the neighborhood here:

(Maybe) use a location-specific descriptor

When I say 'location-specific descriptor' I am referring to a man-made structure (tourist attraction) or a natural formation (beach). If you are by a tourist attraction, you may think about using its name in your Airbnb title. I do not recommend this because the map shows your location within a few blocks. It is not necessary. The guest will zoom in the location and then look for a listing. I typed in 'Wrigley Field' and only one of the top six listings had 'Wrigley' in their title. In this specific case, I do not think most guests will care if they are two blocks or six blocks from the stadium.

If you are next to a natural formation like a beach, it may make sense to call this out. Some guests want to literally be right on the beach. It may be difficult to know this without asking because of Airbnb's map. The listing could be anywhere from in the water to a 15-minute walk to the beach. If you cannot communicate this any other way, you can consider adding it to your title.

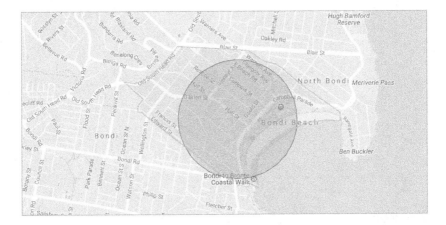

In late 2017 Airbnb began testing a feature that allows Airbnb hosts to choose whether they publicly show their general location with the green circle as is the standard now or their exact location. There are some security risks to consider with showing your exact location, but it may be beneficial for some listings, especially those by a beach, hospital, music venue, or other significant attraction.

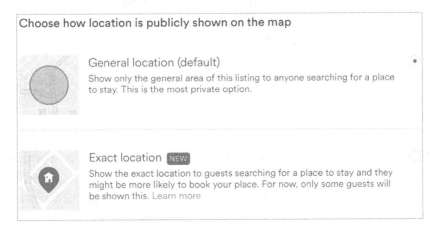

PRO TIP: If you have a large event (sporting event, concert, etc.) coming to town and are unbooked within a few weeks of the event, consider adding the name of it to your title, especially if you are within walking distance. It should garner more clicks from the guest as your title is already in the back of their mind.

CHAPTER 5

Mastering the Text

Key Points

- ▶ Never add fluff, it is useless information in this context.
- ▶ Don't repeat yourself.
- ▶ Keep the presented text as easily digestible as possible.
- ▶ Only present information the guest needs prior to making a reservation.

According to Airbnb, only 30% of hosts make use of all available text boxes. This is a mistake. Don't force yourself to add fluff, but something can be added.

> **PRO TIP:** If your property management software (PMS) doesn't allow you to edit all text boxes available to you within Airbnb, change providers.

I will provide the more common bits of text I use when optimizing a listing. I am providing the identical text to give you ideas and help get the creative juices flowing. Don't copy verbatim. Put your own flair into it. But keep it snappy, catchy, and thorough.

Summary

This text is at the very top of your listing just below the title. If the FPG reads anything, it's the summary. The goal is to get the guest excited about booking your listing so present them all the reasons, in easily digestible bits of information, why they should make a reservation before someone else does. I use bullet points here:

- Amount of square feet/meters/acres or floor level (with numbers, they draw attention)
- Private decks, balconies, terraces, rooftops, etc. (If it has 180° views, say so)
- Pools + hot tubs
- Onsite, secured, gated, garaged parking for X vehicles
- How long of a walk or drive to get to downtown
- Fully stocked and equipped kitchen
- Walk/Bike/Transit Score, from WalkScore.com
- Extremely safe neighborhood

> **PRO TIP:** Highlight one or two review snippets throughout the listing: "An incredible house, with gorgeous views and 6-star hospitality!"

The Space

Spillover from the summary section should go in here. The point of the summary is to hook the FPG so they click the 'Read more about the space' link.

Some example text for 'The Space' section:

- *We use only green and organic cleaning materials and supplies to insure that we are doing our bit for the environment.*
- *Onsite washer + dryer* (Note: Huge luxury in some areas of the world which is why it's called out here in addition to the amenities section.)
- *Flexible check-in/out*

Guest Access

Some example text for 'Guest Access' section:

- *Entire space plus building amenities is included in this rental. Please, make yourself at home.*

Guest Interaction

Some example text for 'Guest Interaction' section:

- *I am here for you during your stay, but our level of interaction is up to you. I'm only a phone call or message away. You will be able to self check-in upon arrival.*

Other Things to Note

Some example text for 'Other Things To Note' section:

- *Please remember that you're staying in a house, not a hotel. Please treat the space with respect. If any problems arise, we will do our best to take action ASAP, but there is no one living on-site 24/7.*

The Neighborhood

This and the next section are at the very bottom of the listing, even below reviews and host profile. The guest needs to click another link 'Read more about the neighborhood' to even see it. Avoid listing a million activities the guest can do as your Airbnb listing is not their trip planner. Instead, highlight a single must do.

- *Check out Airbnb's guide to my neighborhood: airbnb.com/locations* (Note: Alternatively, use airbnb.com/things-to-do)
- *Here are my local recommendations: airbnb.com/things-to-do/rooms/[Airbnb Listing ID]*

Getting Around

This text section is at the very bottom of the listing, just above the map.

- *I highly recommend using ride-sharing services:*
  - *For $20 in Uber credit, use my code – [your code here]*
  - *For $20 in Lyft credit, use my code – [your code here]*

PRO TIP: Add a call-to-action here. If the guest has read down this far, they must be interested, but we know Airbnb encourages them to reach out to many hosts: "I want you! Tell me what I can do to host you on your trip." Or, ask the guest to add your listing to their wish list by clicking the heart in the upper-right corner.

House Rules

The guest must click 'Read all rules' to see this bit of text, but they must agree to whatever you put here before confirming a reservation. Only add rules the guest needs to know prior to making a reservation here. Only bullet points work in this text section:

- *If you open it, close it. If you borrow it, return it. If you turn it on, turn it off. If you break it, fix it. If you use it, take care of it. If you make a mess, clean it up. If you move it, put it back.*
- *All guests must have traveler insurance on their own for the duration of their stay.*

The next three sections are only shown to the guest of a confirmed reservation.

Instant Book Confirmation Message

Some example text for this section:

- *Thank you for choosing my listing! Please let me know at what time you plan to arrive on your date of check-in.*

Directions

Do not add your address here. It's already listed just above this section. You can copy your Lyft/Uber credits and suggest the guest use them for a discounted airport ride. You may also suggest EasyCar.com for car rentals as this search engine works globally.

House Manual

Any additional house rules the guest does not need to know before booking can go here. But, ideally, you will have an electronic guidebook.

CHAPTER 6

17 Unconventional Ways to Increase Your Search Rank

Key Points

▶ The goal is to appear in as many search results as possible.

▶ Airbnb is momentum based, you are rewarded for each positive guest experience.

▶ Wish list saves are a driving force for search rank.

Ready for some non-generic ways to give you an edge? I'm detailing 17 advanced strategies to increase your Airbnb search rank. Luckily, advanced does not mean hard to implement. Instead, advanced means few hosts take advantage.

It's no secret that a lot of where your listing appears in Airbnb search rank has to do with your hosting abilities (i.e. 5-star reviews, see Chapter 12: 5 Tips to 5-Star Reviews). The below strategies focusing on making you appear in more search results. The theory is the more your listing appears in relevant search results, the more it will get booked. And, the more it gets booked (with good reviews), the more Airbnb wants more guests to book your place and your Airbnb search rank rises. You see, unlike Google and their search rank, **Airbnb is momentum based**. This is because your Airbnb listing does something for Airbnb that websites in Googles search rank don't do for it: you make Airbnb money. But, it goes deeper than that. If a first-time guest stays at your place and has a bad experience, the likelihood of that guest returning to Airbnb is low. So, you've lost Airbnb a stream of lifetime revenue. However, if you consistently provide a positive guest experience, you are making Airbnb money with every reservation, but you are compounding their future revenues as these guests are likely to return to Airbnb to book their next vacation. And, Airbnb is still in growth mode. Up to 40% of reservations include a first time guest[8].

> NOTE: Just as reviews are super important to your search rank on Airbnb, they're super important to my search rank on book retailer websites. I am deeply grateful for every review and read all of them (probably multiple times).

Additionally, a side benefit of these strategies is getting more wish list saves which directly increases your Airbnb search rank. It's the Airbnb circle of life.

In no particular order:

Add all home safety features

Airbnb wants to mitigate their risk and liability as much as possible. As such, it would make sense for them to give a search boost to listings with all available safety features installed. In fact, you must have both a smoke detector and carbon monoxide detector to qualify as a Business Travel Ready listing. A safer listing is a more profitable listing.

Relax...your cancellation policy

Airbnb has been pushing a flexible cancellation policy. They have even forced it on some hosts. At a point, they were considering charging hosts 4% and 5% if they selected a moderate or strict cancellation policy, respectively. Given how much Airbnb has promoted the flexible cancellation policy, it's plausible they give a boost to listings with flexible cancellation policies. In a recent change to the cancellation policies, Airbnb has said the changes were "to encourage more bookings—especially for more flexible listings"[9].

---

8   blog.atairbnb.com/guest-onboarding/
9   blog.atairbnb.com/guest-cancellation/

Lower your minimum stay requirement

Every day you lower your minimum stay is going to result in your listing appearing in more search results. Think about it: if your minimum is three nights, you're missing out on guests searching for only one or two nights. I advocate one-night minimums. This will require you to scrutinize guest profiles more (Refer to Chapter 32: How to Identify Problem Guests Before They Book).

> **PRO TIP:** You can use PriceLabs to keep your minimum at 2+ nights, but use their 'Orphan Night' setting to have the software automatically update your calendar minimum night if there's an unbookable night based on your current settings. For example, if you have a two-night minimum with an open day on Wednesday, then PriceLabs will create a special rule in Airbnb to allow only this day to be booked as a single night. Additionally, you can auto set a price increase of X% to avoid the guest who wants to throw a party (the most commonly cited concern over single-night minimums). Flip to Chapter 25: PriceLabs, Smart Pricing Tool for my review and guide on PriceLabs.

Eliminate your maximum stay requirement

If possible, completely remove maximum night requirements. Some hosts worry that the guest will stay because, in some areas, a guest would have tenant's rights if they stay more than 30 days or so. This is like a shark attack because it's incredibly rare, but each time it happens, it makes it to the news making it appear more common. You should be vigilante about these types of guest, but not significantly change your strategies.

Increase your booking window

I advocate opening your calendar to '12 months into the future' when possible. Obviously, you'll appear in more search results. You can also charge a premium if a guest wants to book 3+ months out.

If you do not have a good handle on your areas special events (i.e. conferences, concerts, etc.), then I recommend three or six months out as savvy guests are likely to book up Airbnb listings early when unscrupulous hosts haven't updated their prices.

Lower your pricing

At first, this appears to be 'duh', but I see so many hosts over value their homes resulting in abysmal occupancy levels (sub 30%). No matter where you are in the world or what season it is, if you're ever below 50% occupancy in a month, you're doing it wrong. Lower your pricing in increments of 10% and wait 7 days. Again, the lower your price, the more search results you'll appear in. Airbnb favors more economical listings so lowering your price has the added bonus of a search boost, even a small price decrease of $10. For those hosts starting with really high nightly rates ($200+), you'll experience exponential growth in search results every $15 you lower your rate.

A study from early 2017[10] showed Airbnb heavily favors lower priced listings. This makes sense as we know Airbnb's Smart Pricing keeps hosts calendars cheap because price is one of their greatest advantages over traditional hotels.

Airbnb pricing hack

Refer to Chapter 8: Pricing Hack For More Views for details, but it's a simple strategy that virtually guarantees you more views. You have to connect to a third-party pricing partner. I recommend PriceLabs. (The best alternatives are Wheelhouse and Beyond Pricing.)

Add places of interest to your guidebook

Add popular tourist destinations to your guidebook because these locations are searchable within Airbnb.

Where	When		Guests	
Golden Gate Bridge, San Francisco, CA, Ur	Check In	→ Check Out	1 guest	⌄ Search
Golden Gate Bridge San Francisco, CA, United States				
Golden CO, United States				

Turn your sofa into a bed

Even if it's not a sleeper sofa, if you include it as a bed within Airbnb, you will appear in more search results and be able to charge more. Keep in mind, the more guests you squeeze into one listing, the louder it will inevitably get so you'll have to weigh your options. Party Squasher measures the number of wireless devices in your home. NoiseAware measures the decibel level. Use **OPTIMIZE** at checkout for 20% off both products. Refer to Chapter 28: NoiseAware and Party Squasher, Noise Monitoring to read about my experience with both.

Ensure your listing is up-to-date

Airbnb adds sections without telling anyone. They did this recently with the 'People who clean my listing are paid a living wage' checkbox under extra charges sub-heading in the pricing settings.

> ☑ People who clean my listing are paid a living wage. Learn more.

They basically leave it up to the host to figure it out. Let's turn this into an advantage by checking regularly and staying ahead of the curve. Add this to your as-needed re-optimization strategy (see Chapter 11: How To Re-Optimize Your Listing). Regarding amenities, 'Laptop friendly workspace' often is left unmarked, but should be marked off for 99% of listings. Other amenities that are often missed: Lock on bedroom door, family and kid friendly, and Wi-Fi.

Smoking allowed

I recommend marking this off if you allow guests to smoke anywhere on the property like a patio or backyard. Most smokers don't smoke inside their own home so this is an exception and not the rule anymore. You can and should clarify in the listing, typically under house rules where is and where is not ok to smoke. Smokers are often aware of these special rules and check for them. Often, especially in apartments, the host requires the guest to step onto the street to smoke. This would be a no smoking listing as you need to entirely exit the space to smoke.

Note: This will disqualify your listing from being Business Travel Ready so check to see if you qualify (many listings do not). If you are not in an area where business travelers frequent (i.e. big cities or near-by large corporate headquarters), then this makes no difference for you.

Be suitable for events

If at all possible, mark off 'Suitable for events' (Related: Chapter 16: Make Your Airbnb Event Ready). Guests looking to use your space for a photoshoot or event will often select this filter. Note: Splacer and Peerspace are the Airbnbs for event space. Additionally, you can charge more for commercial uses of your space. I had a start-up shoot a product on my rooftop and I was able to charge two nights. There were six of them in my home, but only for five hours and they were all respectful of the space.

More wish list saves

Within each listing, the guest has the option to save you to their wish list. Airbnb recently confirmed[11] wish list saves directly affect search ranks. Ask your family and friends to save your listing to their wish list and share to your social media accounts including Facebook, Twitter, and Google+. By doing this, you are creating backlinks to your own Airbnb listing, to the Airbnb website, and driving views to your listing. All of this likely results in bonus wish list saves as more people see your listing.

Recently, Airbnb has moved the location to the upper-right portion of the listing and no longer shows the amount of wish list saves. How-ever, Airbnb still tracks this metric.

---

11   blog.atairbnb.com/search/

Add a self check-in option

First, you have to have a self check-in option to be a Business Travel Ready listing[12]. Second, adding this allows you to appear in more search results because this is a heavily selected option under amenities filters. Think about it, after you travel for up to 24 hours, do you want someone to greet you and ask you a bunch of questions and show you how different things work in the listing? Probably not. You'd probably like to unwind.

Allow pets

This one is self explanatory. Refer to Chapter 15: Turning Your Space into a Pet-Friendly Listing for details.

Speak more than one language

Learning a language has now become directly profitable for you to do. A guest is allowed to search by the language the host speaks. This definitely ups your search rank because everyone in the world does not speak/does not prefer to speak English. If you, your significant other, or your housemate speak another language, definitely list it. But only if this person is reasonably available to answer inquiries.

Add a 1% discount

It's speculation, but so is most everything when it comes to search rank, Airbnb may favor listings with discounts. If you are opposed to weekly/monthly discounts, try adding 1% for each option. We know that lowering your price directly affects your search rank so it will help for that reason, but maybe a little bonus too. It's worth a try.

> PRO TIP: Remember to remove discounts in high season to maximize your revenue.

---

12   www.airbnb.com/help/article/1185/what-makes-a-listing-business-travel-ready

CHAPTER 7

Pro Tip: 3 Pros + 2 Cons

Key Points

▶ Don't neglect the relevant negatives of your listing. Instead, identify them to properly set your guest expectations.

▶ List three things guests love about your listing and two things guests don't love about your property.

▶ Don't force yourself to think of negatives. Always consider the cost/benefit of listing a negative.

I have to give credit to Chip Conley, former Airbnb executive and founder of Joie De Vivre, for this Airbnb pro tip. He teaches it in his Hospitality Moments of Truth class[13]. It's all about managing guest expectations when it comes to the success of your listing. In short, **if you portray a 5-star listing and deliver a 4-star listing, you'll get a 3-star review.**

When a host sets out to create a listing, they often do a great job of identifying the positives. After all, they're trying to sell their listing to an FPG. They're in the sales mindset which often times overlooks any downsides. This is a powerful short-term strategy that may come back to haunt them with negative reviews. Even one negative review could haunt you for months. That's because **negative reviews are more important** to an FPG than the positive ones. Think back to the last time you searched Airbnb as a guest. Did you perk up when you found a negative review and read it fully, but skim over many of the positive reviews?

---

13 www.airbnb.com/meetups/hkxak5p3t-hospitality-moments-of-truth-class

The listing could look great in the photos and text, but if the guest arrives to a home 10 feet from a busy freeway entrance, they're going to feel slighted. It's likely the guest mentions this in their review and leaves a less than 5-star review.

How do you get around this situation?

First, I advise hosts to **limit the flowery language** in their listing description as it does not encourage a guest to make a reservation and might make the guest miss some important info. Instead, focus on communicating the most amount of information to the guest in the least amount of text. Often this means a bullet point format.

• • •

Don't force yourself to think of negatives.

• • •

Second, in the 'About this listing' section, **list three things guests love about your listing and two things guests don't love about your listing**. This will force you to think of things a guest might not like about your listing and to be up front about it. You'd rather pass on a guest who's not a good fit than book them for the extra revenue and a negative review. And, who better to decide they're not a good fit than the guest before reaching out to you?

A Word of Caution

Don't force yourself to think of negatives. If you have a run-of-the-mill, standard home with not many exciting features but not any real downsides, skip this.

Additionally, **avoid listing negatives that only effect a small group of guests**. Living above a bar that stays open until 2am on Friday and Saturdays is a negative for the majority of guests. As this is a predictable and regular event, mention it in the listing. However, having a neighbor who throws a party once a year that goes until 6am and takes up all the street parking is not something you should mention. It is not predictable and it is rare. If you rent out your downstairs and have kids upstairs that make noise occasionally, you'll want to consider whether or not to put this in your listing. Putting something as innocent and straightforward as 'I live upstairs with two young children who occasionally make some noise' could be read as 'There's going to be a bunch of noise from kids upstairs, pounding footsteps all day, no sleep at night.' In this case, if the noise is occasional, I would leave it out, try to control the noise, and test to see if this is effecting your reviews.

Some items, like health and safety, should be disclosed at all times no matter how many guests it effects.

CHAPTER 8

Pricing Hack for More Views

Key Points

▶ You must connect to a third-party pricing partner to use this strategy.

▶ It involves lowering your base price in Airbnb by 10-15%. This is the price shown to guests who are searching without dates.

▶ Ensure your base price is not being used in your calendar if you use this strategy.

T here's a little known Airbnb pricing hack amongst Airbnb pros that virtually guarantee more views and reservations. **This pricing hack only works when you're connected to either Airbnb's Smart Pricing (with one exception) or an intelligent pricing partner** (I recommend PriceLabs, but Wheelhouse and Beyond

NOTE: Airbnb is constantly tweaking and testing. They are testing out different calendar and pricing display options at the time of publishing which will affect the applicability of this strategy and/or the website screenshot images will be different than they appear on your computer. Testing does not guarantee this strategy will disappear. Many times in the past Airbnb tests something and ditches it. The overall goal with this strategy is to ensure your displayed price (when no dates are entered) is lower than your daily calendar rates. As always, please email me at Danny@OptimizeMyAirbnb.com for clarifications.

Pricing are two fine alternatives; See Chapter 25: PriceLabs, Smart Pricing Tool on my review of PriceLabs).

A third-party pricing partner (or intelligent pricer) is software that connects to your Airbnb and gives the host more control over their calendar prices. Most of these tools also offer additional functionality that Airbnb does not and the provided prices are more in line with host expectations.

The strategy has to do with the base price in Airbnb and whether or not it's being used in the calendar. Typically, when you connect your account to Smart Pricing or a third-party pricing partner, the base price is ignored in favor of the 'smart' daily pricing. If this is the case, the hack quite simply is to lower your base price 10-15% below your minimum.

Why?

When you're connected to either Smart Pricing or a third-party pricing tool, your base price is only shown in search results to guests who have not inputted dates, which happens often. **What you are doing is enticing these guests to click on your listing which shows an artificially lower price.** Once they're in, they'll fall in love with your perfectly optimized listing and create a reservation.

Kim and Rob's listing ranks #1 in search results in San Francisco (yes, they've been optimized). Below is a screenshot of an example search of San Francisco without any dates entered, only city and number of guests. The FPG would see a price of $155/night. This is slightly lower than their typical rate of $175/nt.

Since the listing ranks high, has a great cover photo, great reviews, a great title, and is **cheaper than the competition**, the guest would likely click to see more.

• • •

Since the listing ranks high, has a great cover photo, great reviews, a great title, and is cheaper than the competition, the guest would likely click to see more.

• • •

Now, the guest falls in love with the listing because the photos are captivating and the text is clear and concise. They enter their dates to see the pricing is actually $175/nt.

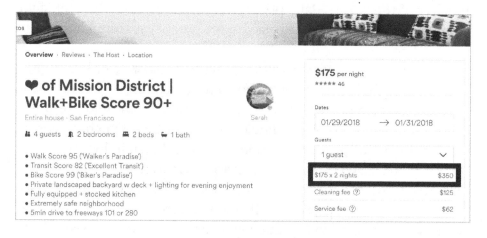

What's an extra $20 per night? They've already searched around and decided on your listing. Plus, 'It's a vacation, we can splurge a bit!', they'll rationalize.

Alternatively, this host is doing it backward. An FPG searching without dates would see $155 per night (upper-left) when, in fact, their true price is much lower at $113 per night (when searching within calendar). This host should lower their base price to $105 or less.

An Exception

You need to ensure that your base price is never being used in your calendar. If it is, someone could book (especially if you're on Instant Book) at a bargain price.

An example is if your chosen smart pricing tool only updates your calendar for a limited number of days (i.e. the next 90 days), then you need to adjust your calendar availability within Airbnb (i.e. in this example, to three months).

This is a rather complex strategy due to the variables and having to use a pricing tool to accomplish it. However, it is worth its weight in gold due to the increased clicks you'll get which has a positive effect on your search rank.

CHAPTER 9

Let's Talk About Revenue Management

Key Points

▶ Connect to a third-party pricing tool.
▶ Understand how far in advance the average guest books in your market and base your calendar occupancy goals off that.
▶ You still need to monitor your prices weekly and adjust your base price accordingly.

D o you want to make more money from your Airbnb listing? Silly me, of course, you do.

Do you use Airbnb's Smart Pricing suggestions? Do you use a third-party pricing tool like Beyond Pricing, PriceLabs, or Wheelhouse? Do you not know what I'm talking about so far?

Airbnb revenue management is a function of two things: rates and occupancy. Your aim is to achieve maximal numbers for both. I'm going to walk you through the three pricing methods first, then my strategy.

There are three methods when it comes to Airbnb revenue management or calendar management. The first method sets one price for the entire year. The hosts who use this method may increase their price on the weekends and for the most popular events. This group is performing poorly at calendar management and missing lots of opportunities for revenue maximization (I'll explain why below).

The next group is using Airbnb's Smart Pricing tool because Airbnb told them it's the best thing since sliced bread. It's free, updates automatically, and based on Airbnb's data. What could go wrong? Hosts quickly realize the prices are low. This is because Airbnb's goal is to put 'heads in beds'. They'd rather give you 100% occupancy at a lower price, then 80% occupancy at a much higher price. Additionally, this tool comes with extremely minimal functionality.

The third group is using a third-party intelligent pricing tool. (My recommendation is PriceLabs, Beyond Pricing, or Wheelhouse). You want to be in this group. As an Airbnb property manager trying to make the most money for my hosts, I had no idea about all the various conferences in San Francisco throughout the year, not just Dreamforce in the fall, until I started using these tools.

Let's say you're already connected to one of these tools or, you're planning to be connected. Now what? These tools aren't a 'set it and forget it' kind of tool. You've got to monitor your future occupancy rates. Most hosts are concerned with what they'll get per night and their minimum. It doesn't matter what you think you can get or what you want your minimum to be. **Airbnb is a true market in that the market will tell you what your listing is worth, not the other way around.** The typical Airbnb host does not raise their price enough for highly demanded dates and does not lower enough for low demand dates. If you want to charge $200 per night and you're at 20% occupancy over the next 30 days, you're leaving money on the table. If you're curious what your space is worth, I've assembled a few calculators[14] from around the web.

My strategy assumes the host wants 100% occupancy at the highest rate possible. Occupancy is defined as the number of nights paid for by a guest. To achieve this, I have occupancy targets for 7, 14, 30, 60, and 90 days out. The vast majority of guests don't book

> • • •
>
> Airbnb's goal is to put 'heads in beds'. They'd rather give you 100% occupancy at a lower price, then 80% occupancy at a much higher price.
>
> • • •

---

14   optimizemyairbnb.com/airbnb-calculator/

more than 90 days out. Those targets are 100%, 80%, 50%, 30%, and 15%, respectively.

These targets change by the market. If the average guest in market A books on average 30 days out and the average guest in market B books on average 60 days out, I would want a higher occupancy at 30 days out for market B. Here's another way to think about it: If the average reservation comes at 30 days out for market A, then only 50% of the available reservations are left to be booked within 30 days out from the reservation (In market B, this would be at 60 days out). So, around 30 days out for market A, I would want a 50% occupancy rate. Then, I'll set the other expectations accordingly.

Timeframe	Occupancy Target
7	100%
14	80%
30	50%
60	30%
90	15%

I regularly monitor and adjust based on my real occupancy. **If my occupancy moves above my target, I raise my prices. If my occupancy dips below my target, I lower my prices.** The amount I lower/raise depends on how different my real occupancy is to my target occupancy, but a general recommendation is to raise/lower in 10% increments. All of the recommended pricing tools above crunch the occupancy numbers for you.

One of my favorite features of these tools is the automatic lowering of your rates if your calendar is open within the next week or so. This feature is hugely beneficial because a room marked down by 25% is better occupied than vacant given the fixed costs.

PRO TIP: Your base price is what you would charge on an average night in an average month. This will fluctuate up and down throughout your hosting career. As it relates to third-party pricing tools, this is the number you will update that effects your entire future calendar rates.

Keep in mind, each intelligent pricing tool has their own set of unique tools.

Regardless, you still have to monitor because one two-week reservation can throw everything out of whack.

In summary, **your rate is based on your occupancy. The market sets your occupancy.** Create occupancy targets over certain future timeframes, or use mine, and compare your actuals. Raise your price if you are over occupied and vice versa.

CHAPTER 10

Why You Should Respond to Guest Reviews + How

Key Points

▶ Shows host engagement to FPGs.
▶ Allows host to highlight one or two positive aspects of a lengthy positive review.
▶ Allows hosts to respond to negative review without calling attention to it.

It surprises me how few hosts actively respond to their Airbnb guest reviews. The above three reasons are why I recommend all my hosts respond to reviews. But, there is a bit of science to it.

First, you don't need to respond to every review. But, you should respond to most even if it's just a "Hi [guest name] – Thanks for the five-star review!" **Responding to reviews shows FPGs that you're an engaged host who reads and cares about their reviews.**

Second, we know that guests don't read, right? Right. But, some guests like to leave lengthy reviews. In this case, **cherry pick one or two aspects of the review to highlight in your response.** Did they mention the really nice view or how central your location is? This is your opportunity to review yourself based on a guest review. The FPG is more likely to read your response and synopsis than the entire review. This is really powerful when the review starts positive and then lists a few negatives. The FPG will likely scan the first line for negative words, not find any and go down to read your succinct response,

therefore, missing the slight negative altogether! See my example below where a guest left a lengthy and mostly positive review with a minor, slightly negative point. In the response, notice the slightly, negative point was ignored and the positive was emphasized:

Third, it's **necessary to respond to negative reviews to briefly
address the issue and how it was resolved.** A FPG doesn't want to
read about your defensiveness towards the situation, only about how it
was resolved. And, since you're already responding to positive reviews,
you won't call added attention to it. Alternatively, see below for how it
looks when you only respond to the negative reviews (Yes, this example of what not to do is from my listing):

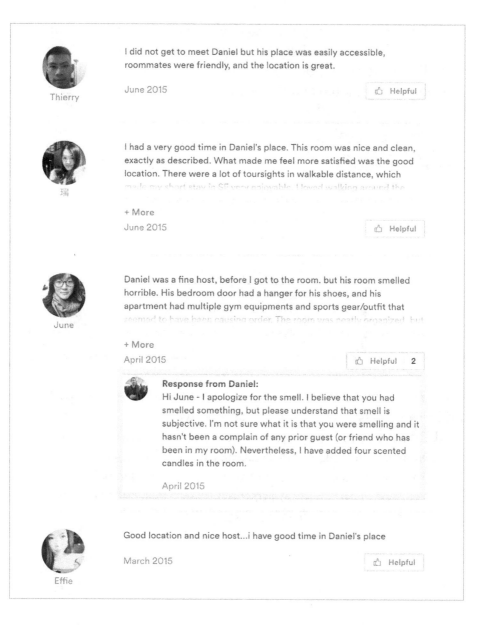

Pretty obvious, right?

Remember, all of your responses should be short and sweet, even the negative ones. **The rule of thumb is no more than two sentences or half the guest review, whichever is shorter.**

CHAPTER 11

How to Re-Optimize Your Listing

Key Points

- ▶ If your occupancy is adequate, skip this chapter until you need it.
- ▶ If your bookings suddenly stop after a certain date, you need a price adjustment.
- ▶ A sparsely booking upcoming calendar is a great indication of a needed re-optimization.

First of all, if it ain't broke, don't fix it. If you have sufficient calendar occupancy, then just let it roll.

Second, ignore your rank. Unlike Google, Airbnb is moving towards more personalized search results based on the guests prior behavior. This means, the position you see your listing in does not correlate to how other guests will see it. The only thing that matters to you is your occupancy level (See Chapter 9: Let's Talk About Revenue Management).

Third, ignore listing views. Again, it's about occupancy only. With that said, Airbnb probably does take into consideration conversion rate, but their data is so rudimentary (and I'm unconvinced on the accuracy as sometimes mobile and desktop show differences) at this point, I'm forced to ignore it.

One more time: Focus on occupancy. It is extremely measurable. If you do not have occupancy goals, you should stop now and read the chapter referenced above. Generally, during high season, you want to have about 50% of days booked within the next month and 100% within the next 7-10 days.

If your occupancy is fine, then you do not and should not do a thing to your listing as it relates to a mini optimization.

You still want to be updating new settings that Airbnb adds. Sign up for the newsletter on my website (www.OptimizeMyAirbnb. com) to have me update you as to when this happens (plus other neat stuff I find while scouring the Internet for Airbnb stuff). You still want to be removing information for your listing as it becomes irrelevant and adding information as it becomes relevant.

• • •

Focus on occupancy.

• • •

If your calendar has a high occupancy rate and then suddenly there are no more bookings after one day, then you may just need a price adjustment. Maybe you are moving into low season? On average, **you will want to vary your price by 40% throughout the year.** I use PriceLabs and have reviewed them with a how to guide (See Chapter 25: PriceLabs, Smart Pricing Tool).

Please be aware this means you have to be actively monitoring your listings occupancy.

On the other hand, if your listing has a booking here and there with many unbooked days in between, then you very well may need a re-optimization. It happens to the best of us. The good news is that it doesn't take more than 10 minutes and should only happen two to three times per year at most.

How to Re-Optimize Your Airbnb Listing

In no particular order and not to be done all at once (typically, you only need to do 4 or 5 of the below items):

☐ **Change your title.**

☐ **Readjust your Airbnb pricing hack.**

- See Chapter 8: Pricing Hack For More Views – This will need to happen 2 times per year. Once for high season and once for low season. Remember, you want your displayed price without dates to be about 10% lower than your actual price. If you go into busy season without changing your base price, it could be 50% lower than your actual price.

☐ **Revise your listing description.**

- If you have not read your listing in 6+ months, I bet you will be able to write it with significantly fewer words while being more informative. Additionally, things may not be relevant that you added many months ago.

☐ **Change your cover photo.**

☐ **Update the order of your photos.**

☐ **Revisit and edit your photo captions.**

☐ **Add a new review photo.**

- Screenshot your best review and add it to your photos around the 5th photo.

☐ **Go through the entire listing settings.**

- To ensure Airbnb hadn't added something that needs to be filled in. They do this often and you want to show the Airbnb system that you are an engaged host by filling in these new requirements as they become available. Sign up for my newsletter on the homepage of my website for me to update you as to when this happens (plus other Airbnb goodies from my hours of online research).

☐ **Make your space event ready.**

- See Chapter 16: Make Your Airbnb Event Ready

☐ **Appear in more search results.**

- See Chapter 6: 17 Unconventional Ways To Increase Your Search Rank

PART II

Your Offline Hosting Style

CHAPTER 12

5 Tips to 5-Star Reviews

Key Points

- ▶ Set expectations early by highlighting both the positives and negatives and letting guests know they can expect a five-star accommodation.
- ▶ Send a check-in message four days before arrival and a check-out message six hours after check-out.
- ▶ When guest issues arise, act as if the issue is more serious than the guest believes and solve it immediately.
- ▶ Upon check-out communicate to the guest that you plan on leaving a positive review.

Three-percent of all Airbnb hosts are considered Superhosts. One of the metrics to achieving this status is receiving at least 80% five-star overall Airbnb reviews. Any existing host knows how hard and important getting a five-star review is. And Airbnb doesn't help much as there's much confusion on whether a five-star reservation met your expectations or treated you like the Ritz. It's so important that there's a black market for buying and selling five-star reviews. But, if caught, you're likely to get kicked off the Airbnb platform as both a host and guest, so I prefer going about it the legit way. Join me.

I'll cover five points that will ensure you receive a five-star review at least 80% of the time, typically 90%+:

1. Set expectations.
2. Send a check-in message.

3. Integrate the guest.
4. Address issues promptly and seriously.
5. Send a check-out message.

Set Expectations

There are two times I set expectations. First, I make my listing clear and concise. I **highlight the positives that will sell my listing and the negatives** that will help me avoid negative reviews. After all, most negative Airbnb reviews are from guests who weren't a good match for the property. For example, if you live across the street from a police station and hear sirens daily, you should mention it. If the guest wasn't expecting this, it's definitely not a positive and wouldn't bode well for your review. Instead, set their expectations early by telling them about the potential for noise before they book.

The second time I set expectations is upon arrival. I will **let the guest know either in person or with a message that they are staying in a five-star Airbnb** listing. I let them know what this means and that if at any time their experience drops below five-stars, to immediately contact me so I can remedy the situation. A lot of new Airbnb guests come from hotels and their idea of a five-star accommodation is the Ritz. It's not like that on Airbnb. A five-star accommodation on Airbnb is getting what you paid for, having common amenities and fresh linens available, and having someone promptly address any issue that comes up. The price usually represents this.

Check-in Message

A few days before check-in, I send additional details about the listing to the guest through an Airbnb message. Avoid providing all information up front as the guest is likely to ignore it, especially if they booked more than 30 days in advance. I send this message four days before check-in as I've noticed that guests start to send messages around two-three days out, asking for details. I prefer to **beat them to the punch by sending a welcoming email first**. Keep in mind, traveling is stressful, so do what you can to ease the guest's mind. It's essential that the welcome email include a link to an electronic guidebook so the message isn't too long. Refer to Chapter 27: Hostfully, Electronic Guidebooks for my recommended tool and guide.

> **PRO TIP:** Have a friend go through the entire check-in process as a guest would. Ideally the friend is unfamiliar with your property. Every time I have done this, important insights surfaced that surely would have cost me a five-star review.

Integrate the Guest

You want your guest to be settled as quickly as possible in your Airbnb so they can get on with their trip. The electronic guidebook plays a major role in telling the guest about details of the property and:

- Identify nearby frequently visited locations (coffee shop, grocery store, gym).
- Provide local activity suggestions (Nearby parks, Vayable, Groupon).
- Help the guest with local words and phrases.
- Tell the guest how to use public transit or taxis (This is especially important as taxis rip-off travelers which is a terrible experience. The guests experience in the city will likely make its way into your review, either consciously or not).

Address Issues Promptly

The customer is always right. The guest is always right, too. The difference is an unhappy customer may not come back into your store and probably won't leave an online review. But **an unhappy guest will leave a review for all future potential guests to see**. According to Airbnb, about 70% of guests leave reviews[15]. I'm sure this number jumps up when a guest has a bad stay. One unhappy guest can hurt your revenue for months.

When, not if, guest issues arise, you must do two things. One, **resolve the issue as quickly as possible**. Two, **act like the issue is**

---

15   www.quora.com/What-percent-of-Airbnb-hosts-leave-reviews-for-their-guests

bigger than the guest thinks it is. Every guest is different. They all come from different backgrounds. They all have different standards. One guest might think a hair on the toilet seat is not a big deal and flush it, another may think hair is grounds to have the entire house recleaned.

To counteract this unknown, you must act like any issue the guest brings up to you is absolutely unacceptable. If you're just as unreasonable in your response as they are, they're more likely to accept your proposed solution. In the example of the hair on the toilet seat, you would act utterly shocked, like it is totally unacceptable, that you are deeply sorry, that the cleaners will get fully retrained, that you will redo your entire cleaning process, etc. This lets the guest know that you are taking their issue seriously. I'm not telling you to be condescending or sarcastic. **Be sincere**. After all, that hair is not supposed to be on the toilet seat and it is a break in the process on your end.

In the case of a reservation that might result in a negative review, delay leaving your review. After ten days, the guest probably isn't as upset at the hair on the toilet seat. Or, forgo leaving a review at all for that reservation. The guest is less likely to review you, if you do not review them.

Check-out Message

About six hours after check-out, I send a message through Airbnb to the guest thanking them for leaving the place in good shape (no matter what shape they actually left it in). I ask them to provide good and bad feedback directly through the message thread, and I tell them that I will leave a positive review tomorrow when the system allows. **This lets the guest know that we're on good terms, and they'll be getting a positive review**. I don't want to leave any question in their mind as to what kind of review they will get.

Bonus Content: How To Improve Sub-Category Reviews

The overall rating is shown in search and is most prominent, but the guest rates each reservation on six additional attributes. If you are lacking in any of them, here are some tips to boost your ratings! Remember to always refer to prior reviews, especially the private feedback, for improvement clues.

Accuracy: Be sure to describe the positive and the negative aspects of your listing to get the right guests. If expectations are managed from the beginning, you'll be in the clear. Refer to Chapter 7: Pro Tip: 3 Pros and 2 Cons.

Communication: Respond within one hour to all messages, ideally sooner. Communicate relevant check-in and check-out info to the guest timely. Be available through numerous methods (phone, email, text) or provide the guest a local contact who is always available. Refer to Chapter 18: Optimizing and Automating Your Messages.

Cleanliness: Each guest's definition of 'clean' is so wildly different that you have to assume their expectations are high. Make sure there's not even one stray hair in the bathroom. When is the last time you saw a hair in your hotel room? Refer to Chapter 17: Cleaning Team Checklist.

Location: Be transparent about your immediate neighborhood in the appropriate section. If it's not in a gated community, that's ok. Just let the guest know what to expect prior to arrival. Adding an electronic guidebook highlighting local bars, parks, cafe's, grocery stores, etc. is a fantastic idea. Refer to Chapter 27: Hostfully, Electronic Guidebooks.

Check-In: Communicate check-in info to your guest three days before arrival whether that's the code or the number to the person who will be doing the live check-in. Have a friend test your process out to find information gaps. I recommend electronic locks, use OPTIMIZE at SmartLock.Shop (European customers) or RemoteLock.com (U.S. and rest of world) for a 10% discount.

Value: Either lower your price or provide additional amenities like Netflix, bikes, prepaid public transit cards, airport pickup, beach items, kitchen cooking amenities, welcome gift, etc.

CHAPTER 13

Superhost Checklist

Key Points

▶ Provide all standard amenities plus some extra 'surprise and delight' amenities.

▶ Create a strong first impression and stand out from the rest with a welcome gift.

▶ Do not use the listing description to tell the guest what amenities you provide unless they're extra special (100 MBPS Wi-Fi) or common, but missing from your Airbnb (no Wi-Fi).

▶ Recommended products can be found at OptimizeYOURAirbnb.com.

Providing a wide array of non-standard Airbnb amenities to your guests is one of the easiest ways to improve your hosting and obtain five-star reviews. Most guests expect basic amenities they would commonly find in a hotel, but there are many ways to exceed their expectations.

Think of it this way – **what items do you commonly forget to pack on your travels? What 'extras' would make your stay more comfortable or convenient?** Turn your answers into amenities you can offer your guests.

Less than 3% of Airbnb hosts are considered Superhosts. To be an Airbnb Superhost, you must:

• Complete a minimum of 10 check-outs within 12 months.
• Respond to 90% of inquiries within 24 hours.
• Receive a minimum of 80% five-star reviews from prior guests.

- Be reviewed by at least 50% of prior guests.
- Have zero cancellations within the past 365 days.

This checklist will tell you what you need to do with your physical property to get there. It will tell you how to never hear from your guest while they are staying in your home because you have thought of everything. Almost like you have been a guest in a hundred Airbnbs around the world and have thought of everything. Lucky for you, I have and am going to share my experience with you.

I've done a live review for a few of these properties and they can be found on my YouTube channel[16] (Search 'OptimizeMyAirbnb' on YouTube).

Before I move on, I need to clarify that these are not the only things you need to do to be a Superhost. You also need an optimized listing and communication strategy. But, whatever you do, don't do this:

The space

Just totally rehabbed new refrigerator and stove.

All bedrooms have flat screen tv

Tile floors

Located just a few steps away from a city park and within a quick drive to Plymouth Meeting Mall, Route 476 and the PA Turnpike

I DO NOT SUPPLY TOWELS SHEETS BLANKETS OR PILLOWS.

I DONT DO PREVIEWS IF YOU ASK FOR A PREVIEW I WILL DENY YOUR REQUEST.

DONT ASK ME TO CALL YOU YOUR NUMBER IS BLOCKED BY AIRBNB AND I DONT NEGOTIATE PRICING

Interaction with guests

text me if you need me (PHONE NUMBER HIDDEN)

Other things to note

PLEASE READ BEFORE BOOKING!

I purposely do not supply sheets, pillows blankets or towels. In the past, I provided these and I had a small number of guests who could never be satisfied with the quality of these items, so I gave up now it is your problem.

---

16 https://goo.gl/SUZEba

This guide will be broken down by area of the home, except for the...

Welcome Gift

A welcome gift is anything given to the guest upon check-in. I recommend you do not advertise this item. A guest is not going to choose your listing because you offer a free bottle of wine or something else. As Chip Conley says, your hosting style should have a 'surprise and delight' aspect. Leave some things for discovery.

Tangent: A sunset is a great 'surprise and delight' feature. Rarely does a sunset show up nice on the photos, but every host who thinks they have a nice sunset includes the photo in their listing. Let the guest discover this upon arrival. It's unlikely they will book your listing because of a low quality photo of a nice sunset.

This is your chance to get creative and foster a positive first impression (along with the check-in process you've simplified for your guest), below are some examples and what I provide:

- Pre-loaded public transit cards
- City memorabilia
  - If a guest needs to buy souvenirs for friends/family back home, this could save them some time
- Something local and unique (brainstorm!)
  - Airbnb created a local guidebook for San Francisco. I give this to my guests upon arrival
- Airbnb swag (See Chapter 40: Useful Airbnb Links on how to order)
- Fruit bowl
- Airport pickup or discounted airport pickup from a local company
  - This is important! Any way you can smooth the process from airport to front door will bode very well for your review
- Local or freshly baked goods
- Map of the city
  - Put some thought into this. You can do better than a generic tourist map that hotels give out. In Helsinki, my host ran

into a hotel and grabbed their map. It was a nice gesture, but seemed like an after thought. The map wasn't all that useful, either.
- Honortab (honortab.com) provides an app that allows the host to charge the guest for convenience items in the Airbnb like wine, gum, etc. Think the mini-bar in hotels, but for Airbnb.
- A handwritten welcome note
  - This is so rare, it undoubtedly will leave a positive first impression

Note: A house manual or guidebook is not considered a welcome gift as it's a standard item.

Bedroom

Your guest will spend 50%+ time in this room so make it as comfortable as possible.

- Firm + soft pillow options to satisfy back, side, and stomach sleepers'
- Luggage stand with shoe rack
  - Very useful for short-term stays when the guest does not unpack their suitcase
- At least one dozen hangers for a longer-term guest reservation
  - Hotels notoriously never have enough
- Tissues
- Full-length mirror
- Small garbage can (with extra garbage bags)
- Individually wrapped earplugs
- Eye mask
  - As a last resort if you cannot provide black-out shades
- Small lighting option on both sides of the bed
- End table on both sides of the bed
- Hypoallergenic + waterproof mattress cover
  - This is your last barrier to any unwanted liquids and has saved me countless times from having to replace the entire mattress.

PRO TIP: Stockpile a bunch of individually wrapped chocolates or candies and have your cleaner put one on every bed pillow in the house.

Bathroom

This is going to be the second most used room by your guests. Some extra items will save your guest a trip to the store or give them a sigh of relief if they forgot a basic item:

- Hair dryer
  - Doesn't have to be fancy, but you're missing out on $10 per night without one[17]
- Face + hand towels
- Toilet seat adjustability
  - Ensure it will stay up, for the gentlemen. Otherwise, we have to hold the seat up with one hand
- Small garbage can
  - Where am I supposed to put the tissues, Qtips, razors, etc.?
- Ledge to put toiletries
  - It is very annoying when you make your guest balance items on the sink or use the closed toilet seat
- How to work shower faucet for hot water
  - Add to electronic guidebook
- Shelf in shower to place shampoo, etc.
- Shower dispenser (shampoo, conditioner, soap)
- Sufficient water pressure in shower and sink faucet
- Lint rollers
- Q-tips

Kitchen

Most guests staying less than a week (average booking on Airbnb is three-and-a-half days) do not use the kitchen, but if you advertise a fully stocked kitchen, ensure it is. Recently, I stayed in a five-star hotel

---

17　qz.com/810309/you-can-earn-10-more-per-night-on-airbnb-just-by-having-a-hair-dryer/

in Russia (I was not allowed to use Airbnb with my visa) with an entire kitchen and a full refrigerator, but not one thing in any of the drawers. I had to call room service to bring me any item I wanted (including basics like utensils) and they charged me $8 just to open my bottle of wine.

- Recyclable market bags
  - For grocery trips
- Ice trays or ice maker
- Refrigerator magnets
  - These inexpensive items can really make the guest feel right at home rather than in a stranger's house
- Drying disk rack if no dishwasher
- Paper towels or dish rag
- Basic cooking supplies
  - Salt + pepper, oil, wooden spatula, strainer, etc.
- Plastic bags (small, medium, + large)
- Ceramic cooking utensil holder for stovetop while cooking
- Scissors
  - You don't realize how handy until you don't have them; don't allow your guests to open packages with knives and risk injuring themselves.
- Wine glasses + opener
- Quality coffee + coffee maker
  - Keurig has become the go to standard
- Large cutting board
- Frying pan cover
  - At a minimum, one that will cover all sizes of your frying pans.
- If you have a small fridge, ensure the top freezer is accessible without layers of frost built up
- Access to purified water
  - Especially important in countries where drinking from the tap is not ok. You should be providing a source to clean drinking water either via a Brita or a filtration system on your faucet or in your refrigerator.
- Blender

- Cleaning Supplies
  - Believe it or not, some guests clean on vacation, especially during longer reservations.
- Can opener
- Bottle opener

Common Space

After a long day of exploring or networking at a conference, this is where the guest will likely first stop upon entering the home in the evening so make it welcoming, comfortable, and relaxing! **Make it feel like they're walking into their own home.** Better yet, like they're walking into their ideal home.

- Add potpourri near the front entrance (Alternatives: Essential oil, reed diffusers, Glade plug-ins, Febreeze Noticeables, or scented candles)
  - Welcome the guest to a natural fragrance
- Multiple types of chairs
  - One type may not be comfy to a guest who may be working from your home. This has happened to me as a guest numerous times and while I'll buy some items for the house, a chair is usually expensive and hard to get back to the listing.
- Screen door
  - Especially if you live in a warm climate where a guest may want to keep the door open, but prevent flies, mosquitos, and insects from getting inside.
- Smart TV
  - At a minimum size of 30". Make it smart so the guest can access their Netflix account.
- Netflix
  - For $10/month, this is a sellable feature guests want.
  - If your TV is not 'smart' then purchase a Roku device.
- How to work television with remotes
  - A must if you have more than one remote.

○ On/off plus how to access music or games, if applicable. Using photos here are best. Also indicate which channels are in English or how to get to the TV guide.

> **PRO TIP:** The physical guestbook (with a pen) is a lost art form. Provide a high-quality guestbook for your guests to sign or doodle in. It's a great way to add a personal touch with very little maintenance.

Outdoor Space

If you have outdoor space (backyard, front patio, or balcony) ensure it isn't forgotten about. Have your cleaners wipe down the surfaces and arrange the furniture. Have your gardener regularly manicure the grass and flowers. This is a first impression you do not want to miss.

- Bluetooth speakers
  - ○ These went missing from my Airbnb and numerous guests asked about where it is. This is a highly desirable, underrated item.
- Seating
  - ○ Maybe this is obvious, but I have been in Airbnb's with outdoor space, but zero seating.
- Mountain bike or beach cruiser
  - ○ Especially useful if you're in a tourist area or beach town. Check your Bike Score[18] to find out.
- Manicured yard
  - ○ Dead leaves, spider webs, and overgrown bushes are an eye sore.
- Green grass
  - ○ If you have photos with green grass, it should be green upon guest arrival.
- BBQ with available gas or coals
  - ○ Proper grilling equipment
- Picnic umbrella

---

18   www.walkscore.com/bike-score-methodology.shtml

Miscellaneous Amenities

Some items only certain guests will use and only in certain situations, but these are the things that transform you from host to Superhost when the guest thinks 'Oh, perfect! I'm so glad that's here.':

- Extra-wide ironing board with iron and clothes rack
  - Never ever provide a mini ironing board
- International power adapter
  - To limit theft on this item, you might only provide when the guest asks or specifically tell them where to locate it
- Umbrella
- Local newspaper
- Good water pressure throughout (shower and sinks)
- Coat hangers
  - Also used to hang backpacks that guests have usually for a day of exploration
- Desk
  - Ensure it is both long and wide enough for a comfortable position. Specifically, wide enough to be able to setup a laptop stand and keyboard, or about 24".
- Safe
- Double-paned windows or some kind of noise cancelling insolation
  - Silence bothers no one, but noise can drive some people crazy.

CHAPTER 14

Interior Design Tips

Key Points

▶ Interior designed listings are able to charge higher rates and do better during slow season.

▶ Interior design creates powerful photos and can help increase the mood of the guest when onsite.

▶ This chapter contains do-it-yourself tips. See the last section for three professional remote interior design recommendations.

Interior design is truly an art. But, it's also an investment. From my experience, interior designed Airbnb listings, even ones that have done just above the bare minimum, do better all year round than ones with no interior design. It is so important not only for great photos, but for the functionality of the listing, too. I'm seriously impressed with anyone who knows how to do it because I do not. If you're like me, when you read about choosing natural colors, accent pieces, and a variety of textures, your mind goes blank. Ah...uhm...what?

This is why I set out to accumulate all the interior design easy-to-implement tips from the internet and advice from my interior design savvy friends in one place.

Here goes:

- Buy artificial orchids from Amazon. They're cheap and require no maintenance yet will add some color to any room. Alternatively, fake plants work to add color to any room.

- Choose a theme. As you may have noticed, I've chosen Airbnb as the theme of this book cover. This makes choosing colors pretty darn simple.
- Wall hooks. I know, random. But not just any wall hooks, cool wooden wall hooks, trendy wall hooks, or artsy wall hooks. They can add a bit of pazzaz to an entry way (without making it feel cluttered), a bathroom, or bedroom.

- Always use white bed sheets. It's a psychological thing. It's no coincidence that hotels only use white sheets. The communicate cleanliness. You can add pillows or a blanket for some color.
- Add a piece of framed artwork on the wall – the larger the better.
- Put outside furniture, inside. Basically turns you into an artist with one move. You might need a second opinion to ensure it works, but this is a viable option most of the time.
- Use super bright white paint with a matte finish on the walls and ceiling. Using the same color for both blurs the lines between wall and ceiling making the space feel larger.
- Lay a doormat in the front entryway and to any balconies, patios, or backyards. It doesn't have to be anything special, just a mat with 'welcome' is sufficient.
- Add extra decorative pillows onto sofa, chairs, beds, etc. This is a great place to add some color, but you'll need to make sure it works. You can use this color wheel to ensure you're at least on the right track when it comes to matching: goo.gl/5gbgrY.
- Add a wreath or a decoration to the front door.
- Ditch the curtains. It'll open up the room a bit. Instead, add roller shades.

- Increase your lamp game. Each bed should have a lamp on both sides. This is the perfect spot to add a bit of frill because you really can't go wrong.
- Adding a rug to the kitchen, bathroom, living room, or bedroom is easy and can add a bit of color.
- Always make a luggage rack available to your guest. Plus you can get a super cool bamboo or stainless steel one that can spice up your photos.
- Dress up the ceiling lights, possibly add a chandelier or track lighting.
- Open floor plans are great, and so are decor dividers, which can help separate spaces in an effective and interior-designed manner.
- Fan out a bunch of magazines on the dining room table for a homey feel during photos.

Bonus Tips

- When in doubt, get furniture that you can "see through" meaning something with lots of open spaces and not bulky, like such:

- Careful with hallways. Don't add much, if anything, to avoid a cluttered feel.
- Mirrors make all rooms seem bigger, lighter, and more open; anchor all mirrors no matter what!

- Don't have much, if any, personal items out. If it relates to you and you alone, remove it.

Remote Interior Design Providers

- **Mylinh Tran** (www.AmbienceofEden.com)

- **Decorilla** (www.Decorilla.com)

- **Laurel & Wolf** (www.LaurelandWolf.com)

- **Havenly** (www.Havenly.com)

At the end of the day, if you're trying to run a successful Airbnb, you must do at least a little to improve the look and function of your home. The above tips can be implemented by anyone. However, if you want to get more detailed, post a request for an interior designer to your friends on Facebook. Tell them you are looking to spice up your Airbnb. The great thing about interior design is that many people are good at it and enjoy doing it as a hobby!

CHAPTER 15

Turning Your Space into a Pet-Friendly Listing

Key Points

▶ Becoming pet-friendly increases your guest demand thus increasing your nightly rate and occupancy.

▶ You face significantly less competition among travelers with pets.

▶ Airbnb guests traveling with pets stay longer and are more likely to leave positive reviews.

▶ To prepare, purchase a potty pad, pet fence, and treats. Also, add the nearest dog park to your guidebook.

Pet-friendly Airbnb listings are so unpopular among hosts that it could net you some serious dough if you opened up your listing to allow pets. Airbnb has even added a filter specifically for pet-friendly listings.

According to TripAdvisor, 53% of travelers with pets, travel with their pets[19]. That's a missed opportunity. In my experience, only about 5% of listings have valid reasons for not being pet-friendly. On the other hand, most hosts cite owner control (or, lack thereof) as the reason they would not allow pets rather than the pet itself. This is interesting, but my recommendation is to make your home pet-friendly and here's why:

---

19   tripadvisor.mediaroom.com/US-press-releases

Less Competition

It's no surprise that fewer homes are pet-friendly. It is surprising at how few actually are. I did a quick experiment and searched entire homes for two guests in San Francisco with the pet-friendly filter on and a price range of $125-$150. I got 45 rentals to choose from. Keep in mind, this is all of San Francisco.

Then, I removed the filter and unsurprisingly got 300+ available rentals, the highest number Airbnb shows. If it were exactly 300 rentals, that would mean only 15% are pet-friendly. I know San Francisco has about 7,000 listings. This would represent 0.6% (45/7000). However, by my rough estimation, I think that no more than 3% of Airbnb rentals are pet-friendly in any given market. This means you're going to have significantly less competition when it comes to travelers with pets. Less competition equals higher occupancy and higher rates.

Increased Rates

It's typical, even normal, for a pet-owner to pay more when they bring their pet. I've even seen listings that specify add an extra $50/night fee for guests with pets. At a minimum, the security deposit is increased. **If you increase your demand, your occupancy and pricing goes up, too.**

Higher Occupancy

This all makes sense, right? If there's less competition, you can charge higher rates and expect higher occupancy rates. You open yourself up to more renters when you accept pets. About 40% of Americans own pets, let's assume that a quarter travel with their pets semi-regularly, that's 10% of travelers you're missing out on by not being pet-friendly. Additionally, this 10% of travelers are trying to fit themselves into 3% of Airbnb listings.

This is especially important when it comes to slow season in your area. If you're able to get an extra five nights per month during these slow times, that's a huge bump to your revenue.

Long Stays

There are those folks who travel with their pets 100% of the time. But for the rest of us, we'd probably only consider traveling with our pet if we are to be gone for an extended time, say a month or more. This is the Airbnb host dream, to book a guest who needs a long-term stay.

Better Reviews

This is my theory based on experience, but I'm guessing owners of pets leave a higher proportion of five-star reviews. They understand that most hosts don't allow pets and so are grateful to have found a listing where they can be accompanied by their pooch. Of course, you still have to be a good host offering a positive experience.

Considering a pet-friendly Airbnb?

There are a few things you should do to your listing if you decide to become pet-friendly. If you don't have an outdoor space, it would be wise to purchase some indoor potty pads. Ensure nothing edible is dog-head level or lower. Anything fancy or easily breakable should be moved above this level, too. You should invest in an indoor pet fence in case there is a room or two that is still off-limits to pets. You should also consider buying pet treats as your extra 'wow' factor and add the nearest pet park to your guidebook.

CHAPTER 16

Make Your Airbnb Event Ready

Key Points

- ▶ This is a strategy to add another stream of revenue to your space and to fill days during low season.
- ▶ A host of benefits including no slow season, limited cleanup, no kitchen usage, higher profit margin, less wear and tear, and extra tax deductions.
- ▶ The potential downsides are insurance, permits, inspections, and zoning laws.

We are all familiar with the dreaded 'Parties and events allowed' question within the Booking Settings of Airbnb.

It seems to be an automatic no for us. NO. In my experience, 95%+ Airbnb hosts do not say yes to this option. Similar to the last chapter about why we should make our Airbnb listing pet-friendly, let's put aside the common sentiment and explore the possibilities. After all, we could be unknowingly missing out on large payouts for what are often single-day affairs. And, I feel terrible about that.

Understandably, a lot of Airbnb listings are not event space suitable for one reason or another (size, safety, location, etc.). But, a lot are and I want to at least introduce us to the option of making your Airbnb event ready. This post is written under the context of using this strategy to help add an additional stream of revenue to our Airbnb business or as a way to earn extra revenue during the slow months.

When I say 'event', I am referring to a professional or semi-professional event with commercial purposes. I am not referring to a teenager wanting to throw an after party at our homes – typically the first thing Airbnb hosts think of. Many of these bookings are from professionals where we will be working with top creatives in their field and other people who love cool spaces.

Let's see if I can convince you to turn your Airbnb into an event ready Airbnb.

No Slow Season!

Space for events, commercials, movies, etc. are needed year-round.

Increase Your Demand + Occupancy

With every selection of 'yes' on Airbnb, we increase our potential market size. An increased market size is another way of saying an increased demand which means more money.

Have a hot tub? In certain instances, some guest will not book without a hot tub and others would prefer one.

Allow self check-in? Some guests prefer to meet in person, but many more prefer an automated process with the option of a live check-in. After you have been flying for 12 hours, do you want someone talking to you for an hour? No. NO.

If we allow parties and events, it is one more stream of revenue (i.e. guests) looking at your space.

Increase Revenue

The one benefit of allowing parties or events is that **we can generally charge a commercial rate.** Reasonably, twice our normal rate. According to Peerspace, the average payout is $1,000 and most listings receive upwards of 10 inquiries per month.

For those of us hosting only when we are on vacation because we need our home to sleep in, this allows us to rent out during the daytime while we are at work thus bringing in another stream of revenue while we are already earning a salary at work.

Less Wear and Tear

For one, they are not sleeping the night. An event venue is a day/evening time activity. Some events may last only a few hours. That is twice the nightly rent for 1/6 the time.

People throwing events and parties are professionals. We can quickly understand the nature of the party or event with a few questions. Obviously, we may think twice about a DJ all-night rager, but most events are not like this. Barring these types of events, the event organizer will usually be rolling items in and using protection on the floors.

Limited Clean Up

Professional event planners include cleanup of the space. This means our place is going to be clean after your guests check out.

No Kitchen Usage

Typically, an event is not going to use the kitchen. They will either not be serving food or bring their own. Unless we have a chef's kitchen, it will not be used.

Considerations When Turning an Airbnb into an Event Venue

If not already done as part of our existing Airbnb hosting activities, it is extremely wise to **lock up any valuable or irreplaceable items.**

Expect a lot of people. If someone wants to shoot a commercial, they will need a staff of people helping make this happen.

If the event is selling alcohol on premise, you **may need additional permits.** If they sell to minors, you may be held liable.

A home inspection by our local government may be required. This can uncover costly issues we need to fix before they issue us proper documentation.

Visit your tax accountant because certain additional items may now be deducted from your tax return.

Even though guests are not sleeping over, we are still in a legal quagmire. We could violate zoning laws or the building certificate of occupancy.

Extra insurance may be needed. See Chapter 37: Airbnb Host Insurance Information and Chapter 38: Q+A with Proper, Airbnb Insurance.

How To Turn Your Space Into An Event Venue

In addition to selecting 'Parties and events allowed' on Airbnb, we will want to use a specialty website that caters to folks looking for these types of spaces. There are a many options available if you search 'book event space', but I recommend Peerspace (prsp.ac/2udGTtn) for a few reasons (Splacer (www.splacer.co/) is also a well-known company).

- Peerspace provides insurances against damage and liability[20].
- Their interface is similar to Airbnb so you should feel right at home.
- They are based in San Francisco, just like our favorite company, Airbnb.
- They are legit according to Forbes[21].

Here is how it works, look familiar?

How it works

1 Create a listing

It's free and easy to list. We'll help you discover new uses for your space and optimize your listings to increase reservations. You determine your availability, and decide your hourly pricing.

2 Respond to inquiries and requests

Within hours you'll receive inquiries from qualified potential guests. When a booking request is submitted, you can easily respond and accept bookings.

3 Create a memorable experience

We'll send you all the confirmed details and remind you to greet your guests. If your guests need additional services, our Concierge team will be here to help.

4 Get paid and earn a 5 star review

After your booking, you and your guest will review each other. Being attentive on the day of will help you earn glowing feedback from the community. A secure payout will be directly deposit to your bank account.

---

20 peaceofmind.peerspace.com/
21 goo.gl/h93kFD

Make the space plug and play for the guest. For meetings, have tables and chairs, strong Wi-Fi throughout, and a screen for sharing. Check out a guide the Peerspace team put together to help us transition from Airbnb listing to event space: Showcase Your Space: Perfect Your Listing[22].

Full disclosure: I have not personally used Peerspace, but an Airbnb host who I know well has used them for over a year and speaks highly of them. I have had contact with their team and have experienced nothing but stellar customer service and quick responses to my emails (Splacer did not get back to my two emails). I have also vetted their sites user experience.

---

22   blog.peerspace.com/showcase-your-space-start-improving-your-listings/

CHAPTER 17

Cleaning Team Checklist

Key Points

▶ Cleanliness is the #1 complaint of Airbnb guests.

▶ Hiring a responsible, timely cleaning team will be one of your hardest tasks.

▶ Don't go budget. In this area, you want to hire for quality over price.

▶ A good cleaning team can act as an emergency contact, live check-in help, and replenish consumables.

▶ Recommended apps: Properly (www.getproperly.com) and TurnoverBnB (www.turnoverbnb.com)

Hiring a quality cleaning team is going to one of your most important tasks. When I started my property management company, I negotiated for the cheapest cleaner and then tried to lower their rates even more by guaranteeing them a certain amount of jobs per week. This was the wrong approach. Yes, I got a killer rate on the cleanings, but the quality was not as high as I needed. It wasn't bad, but with Airbnb, it needs to be perfect.

If you hire budget cleaners:

• You will receive lower cleaning ratings.

• You will waste time dealing with upset guests with high cleaning standards (think one stray hair on the toilet seat example).

NOTE: To get this chapter in Word format, click 'Claim Bonus' at www.OptimizeYourAirbnb.com

- You will spend more money on linens as their organization will be lower.

Trust me, hire expensive cleaners as they will save you time and earn you more money in the long run. Below is my full cleaning team checklist. If you don't get cleaning right, you won't get hosting right.

PRO TIP: If you're looking for a cleaner, call a nearby hotel and ask for their best cleaner. Don't say it's for your Airbnb! Cleaners who clean for hotels are more suitable to clean your Airbnb than residential cleaners due to the amount of differences in the job tasks.

You must understand that unless a cleaner has experience with hotels or short-term rentals, the requirements are markedly different than a typical residential cleaning. The checklist highlights these differences, but you should also be aware of them and ensure the cleaner grasps these differences. Higher end cleaners will more efficiently internalize the differences into their daily jobs. Ideally, the cleaners will speak the local language as they are likely to interact with guests. Additionally, if you cannot easily communicate with them, many tasks will be lost in translation and things will go uncommunicated as it will be easier to do so.

The cleaner must be aware of the end product. The end product is a five-star cleaning review. You must ensure the cleaner knows how valuable cleaning ratings are. The better cleaning job, the higher the cleaning reviews, the more reservations, the more money for both you and the cleaner. For this reason, I always choose to work with a local cleaner. If you work with a corporation, the individual cleaner is not incentivized to do a good job as they don't receive any benefit from spending an extra five minutes getting the place presentable for the guest.

Here is the checklist (circles represent items specific to vacation rentals):

The checklist

- [ ] *Proactively check for damage, missing/stolen items, or items left by guests and immediately notify host. Also notify host if excessively dirty.
- [ ] **In addition to the items you are responsible to refill below, it is your responsibility to communicate to host when any of the following supplies are below 25% of capacity: garbage bags, dishwasher detergent, ant spray, air freshener spray, sponges, and laundry detergent.
- [ ] ***Put furniture/pillows/appliances in original placement.
- [ ] ****Where possible, open blinds in rooms to maximize natural light.

Kitchen

- [ ] Wash all dirty dishes or place in dish washer and start cycle.
- [ ] Wipe down inside of oven, microwave, fridge.
- [ ] Sanitize sinks/countertops.
- [ ] Wipe down all appliances/surfaces (including the toaster crumb tray and inside pieces of coffee maker/grinder).
- [ ] Sweep/Vacuum/Swiffer/Mop if needed.
- [ ] Empty dishwasher.
  - Put out clean dish towel.
  - Empty fridge of anything opened or expired except for condiments.
  - Ensure that dishes and silverware already in storage area are clean.
  - Ensure presentation of kitchen items are correct (mugs with mugs, forks with forks, etc.).
  - Refill ice trays and put in freezer.
  - Refill (if needed): paper towels, dish soap, coffee, tea.

Bathroom

- ☐ Remove all items from sink, shower, shelves, racks, etc.
- ☐ Spray all the surfaces at once using a multi-surface disinfectant.
- ☐ Clean toilet (be sure to clean the bottom side and behind the lid).
- ☐ Clean tub.
- ☐ Clean mirror with glass cleaner.
- ☐ Sweep/Vacuum/Swiffer/Mop if needed.
  - ○ Put out one hand towel.
  - ○ Crease toilet paper (goo.gl/eQza8p).
  - ○ Refill: toilet paper, hand soap, shampoo, conditioner, shower gel soap, tissues.

Bedrooms

- ☐ Wipe all surfaces using multi-surface disinfectant.
- ☐ Make beds.
- ☐ Sweep/Vacuum/Swiffer/Mop if needed.
  - ○ Check for stains on sheets or blankets, inform host.
  - ○ Check closets, under bed, and drawers for prior guests personal items that may have been left behind, notify [host] if you find anything.
  - ○ Neatly fold and place two body towels and one hand towel per bed (goo.gl/RTyFww).

Common/Living Areas

- ☐ Wipe down all surfaces, even the shelving that's up high; use glass cleaner where appropriate.
- ☐ Sweep/Vacuum/Swiffer/Mop if needed.
  - ○ Presentation is key. Please create a good first impression for the guest by organizing pillows, chairs, blankets, etc.

- If patio/outdoor space, make presentable with a light clean, sweep, and furniture arrangement.

- Place house manual, local guidebooks, and keys in one obvious location.

Final Check Before Leaving (*Is the house as presentable as it can be for the guests?)

☐ No obviously uncleaned areas (crumbs, marks on walls, etc.).

☐ Dishwasher is empty.

☐ AC/heater turned off.

☐ Stove top/oven is off.

☐ Trash has been emptied from every receptacle and replaced with a new trash bag.

☐ Lights are turned off; windows and doors are locked.

- Plants are watered.

- Proper amount of towels are laid out in bedroom, bathroom, kitchen.

- Household consumable supply levels are full.

- All light bulbs in all rooms are working.

- Doors to bedrooms are open.

Other Notes:

☐ Please use fragrance-free cleaning agents (i.e. avoid Lysol Lemon smell, Bleach, etc.).

PRO TIP: Tell your cleaners to start and end 30 minutes after check-in and before check-out, respectively. This allows you to compromise with the guest as to late check-outs/early check-ins and avoids phone calls from the cleaners who arrived right at check-out time to guests still in the property.

PART III

Your Online Hosting Style

CHAPTER 18

Optimizing + Automating Your Messages

Key Points

▶ Only communicate information to the guest when they need it most.

▶ No message should be more than 100 words, at most. Creating an electronic guidebook is necessary.

▶ Remember to turn off automated messages (and reviews) if you have a bad guest experience.

You write too much. For 75% of you reading this, it is true. Here is the ultimate go to jail card:

Do you send your guest a check-in message that is monstrous? I'm talking 500+ words.

I have received this message as a guest. It's too much. Here is an example (I cut it off halfway through as you will get the point):

Hello Danny!   ⚐
You're trip to LA begins in 2 days! We're excited to be welcoming
you to our apartment. In preparation for your stay, I will be sending the
following important information both through Air Bnb's message
system as well as to the personal inbox of the email you used to sign up
with Air Bnb in case you use multiple emails. It will be from (EMAIL
HIDDEN) and the subject "Your Air Bnb reservation."
The address of the apartment is   , #602, Los
Angeles, Ca 90014. Check in is anytime after 3pm Thursday.
The building has taken steps to make it a more secure and safe place to
stay. Because of the new system at the building, I'll need to know when
you expect to get to the apartment, so I can pass that information on to
the building manager. To get into the building, enter 708 into the
intercom and I will buzz you in. From there, if you arrive between 2-
5pm, you can check in with the building manager in the lobby and get
the fob which you will use to get in the building, up the elevator and to
the roof top area. After 6pm, it will be the security guard that will
check you in. The apartment has an e-lock, code 5270.
The building management require that you check in with them with a
valid photo ID. They can be found in the lobby, Mon-Friday between 9-
5.
The wifi network is: Netgear70
The wifi password is: silenthat700
You should also visit the rooftop area. Take the elevator up to the 12th
floor and then take the flight of stairs up to the roof. You don't need a
key. But maybe bring your swimsuit as there is a hot tub up there.
Please follow all apartment rules there: no alcohol. No glass in the area.
Thank you.
Should you have a car, there is parking for you at Joe's Parking at 807
S. Hill Street. It's a bright orange and yellow building, just 2 blocks from
the apartment building. To gain access to the garage, you will find a
garage key card in the apartment. Please return the garage key card to
the apartment before you leave to avoid being charged $20 to replace
it.
Check out is 11 AM Wednesday, October 26. If you leave before 9AM,
please drop the fob into the old fashioned mail box in the lobby by the
bank of elevators. After 9AM, you can check out with the building

There is a predictable pattern to Airbnb reservations. After understanding this natural flow, I created and optimized a set of messages for Airbnb message automation that saves me 80%+ of my time I
would have used crafting messages, sending messages, and answering
questions. If you implement my strategy, the only questions you will
respond to are specific ones only a handful of guests ask.

PRO TIP: You'll have to respond to guests who ask for a discount in their initial message. If it's a slow season, I usually accommodate. Otherwise, I tell the guest to check back with me one week prior to the requested dates. If the calendar is open at that point, I'll happily honor their discount. I find this the most efficient way to respond to these messages and it offers a safety net for a last-minute booking if the guest holds out.

Below I share my reservation message flow with you. I also share the tools I use to accomplish this strategy. Except for one message as an example, I am not going to share my exact wording as I want to encourage you to create your own messages. Instead, I provide a guideline. If you'd rather have the exact wording for every message, I put together a document for purchase on my website titled Airbnb Message Flow Strategy + Templates. Purchasers of this book can use code OptimizeBook for 50% off.

If you decide to build the messages on your own there is one thing to remember: keep them concise. Most of the messages I have created for this flow are below 50 words.

PRO TIP: If you receive a message simply asking if the place is still available, respond with the following to create a sense of urgency in the guest: "It is available right now. Another guest has reached out, but hasn't booked yet. Are they with your party?" The question is optional, but I believe makes it seem more authentic.

Part of creating a good experience for the guest is knowing what, when, and how to communicate with them.

Here is what NOT to do:

- Do not send any messages in excess of 100 words unless absolutely necessary.
- Do not send check-out info at any time other than near or at check-out time.

- If one out of 100 guests does something you do not like, do not create a rule and make the other 99 read it.
- Do not disrespect the guest's time by making them read things they do not need to.
- Do not treat the guest like a child and repeat yourself unnecessarily.
- Do not create lengthily 'do not do' lists.

Here is what you should do:

Communicate only necessary information to the guest in an effective manner and timely.

I have the following messages prepared and automatically sent to my guests as part of my Airbnb automation strategy:

1. Initial booking inquiry
2. Request to book message
3. Booking confirmation
4. Check-in information
5. One day after check-in message
6. Pre check-out message
7. Post check-out message
8. Review reminder
9. Friends + Family discount offer

Tools you will need to accomplish this strategy:

- Smartbnb (or a PMS of your choice that allows for sending automated messages). Refer to Chapter 24: Smartbnb, Message Automation for my review and how to guide. You can also refer to my YouTube channel for a video guide.
- Hostfully electronic guidebook (or Coral)

Booking Inquiry

If an FPG does not want to Instant Book or send a booking request, they can send an inquiry instead. An inquiry is a message to the host without an intention to book. It occurs when the FPG clicks on the green 'Contact host' link within the listing text.

In this case, I acknowledge receipt immediately and inform them I will address any questions shortly. This comes in handy if I am asleep. I let the guest know this is an automated message. It is a personal preference that has worked for me and I have received no negative feedback related to the decision.

The reason comes down whether of not a guest asks a question within the inquiry. If they do, then an automated message that doesn't address the question seems extremely impersonal. About 40% of reservations are from first time guests who have been told Airbnb is more personal than a hotel from the actual accommodation to the communication with the host[23]. Foster this idea. Be personal.

Request to Book

You will receive a request to book inquiry if you: do not have IB setup, or you have IB setup but your limitations do now allow the guest to use this feature (either you require them to have a verified ID and they do not or you require at least one positive review from prior hosts and they do not).

You have to approve/deny each of these booking requests individually. It should be similar to your booking inquiry message where you're simply confirming availability and that you received the message and will have an answer shortly.

Booking Confirmation

If you manually accept a request or a guest is ready to book and the listing has IB activated, the following message will be sent to the guest upon booking confirmation:

Hi, [guest], and thanks for your reservation!
I will contact you three days before your arrival to make sure that everything is okay on your side, and give you some additional instructions for a smooth check-in.
P.S. This is an automated message, but I do read every message. I'll address any questions shortly.

---

23   blog.atairbnb.com/guest-onboarding

Check-In Information

I send a check-in message four days before arrival with relevant information. I have found that most questions start coming around two and three days from check-in so sending a message on the fourth day before check-in eliminates these extra messages.

In my booking confirmation message, I promised to send this message three days before check-in, but I actually send it four days before check-in to avoid messages like this: "Hey! You said you would send check-in info by now, but I have not received it. Do you mind sending?" Due to time differences, this message is likely if you say three days and send three days before check-in.

This message should be extremely short with no repeated information and a link to your electronic guidebook. The **only time I would repeat information here is when it is of extreme importance** (quiet hours, no smoking, and other generic house rules are not of extreme importance). An example of extreme importance is if you rent out many rooms in one house, you will want to identify which bedroom the guest is to check-in to here.

I use Hostfully (alternate: Coral) for my electronic guidebook. Refer to Chapter 27: Hostfully, Electronic Guidebooks for my review and guide.

Check-Up Message

At 11am, the day after check-in, I send a message to the guest asking how they have settled in. This allows me to address any problems real time to ensure a 5-star Airbnb review. About 75% of the guests do not respond to this message. You may also choose to send this message a few hours after check-in as this is the time the guest is getting used to your house and will have the most questions. I send my check-in message the next day because I do not know when the guest will check-in and I want to let them figure out the small stuff. 90% of issues are easily solvable by the guest (the TV doesn't work because it's not plugged in. I'm serious, these issues arise all the time). The guest will reach out in the other 10% of issues as I've made myself available to them.

Pre Check-Out Message

At 5pm the day before check-out, I will remind the guest of the check-out time and any important specifics they should be aware of. This is a good opportunity to repeat yourself (remember, this info is already in the guidebook) as you are saving the guest the step of opening the guidebook and finding the check-out instructions.

I mention that I hope their stay was 5-star quality. I want my Airbnb guest to know I expect a 5-star review.

Post Check-Out Message

This is the most important message and I believe the cause of the many 5-star reviews I have received and I have earned for the hosts I property manager, all of which are Superhosts. Three hours after their scheduled check-out time, I send the final message related to the actual reservation.

I thank them for leaving the place in good shape. This message goes out regardless of how the guest actually left the place. This is because regardless of how the guest left the space, I still want a 5-star review. I never try to charge the guest an extra cleaning fee except in the most egregious scenarios. With this message, **I am setting the expectations that I am happy with the guest and they will be getting a 5-star review.**

The message is sent before the guest can leave a review in the hope that if they were planning to leave a negative review, they feel bad as I have just thanked and told them they earned a positive review.

> **PRO TIP:** Unlike traditional longer-term rentals, you can rely on your guests in telling you what's wrong with your place. This is beautiful. You should encourage them to do so.

Review Reminder

This goes out only if the guest has not already left a review. Most PMS systems are smart enough to recognize this and not send the message in these cases. About 72% of Airbnb guests leave reviews[24] so this message mostly does not go out. Keep in mind that if the reservation was not positive, you will not want to pester the guest about leaving a review which might not be 5-stars. **5-stars is an A+, 4-stars is an F-.**

> NOTE: Speaking of review reminders...I'd like one, too. Please show your support by leaving me a book review. I promise to read it.

Friends + Family Discount Offer

To increase occupancy during slow season, I extend an offer proactively to prior guests and their friends and family to stay at my listing for a discount. Just remember to turn this message off if the guest was not pleasant.

If your area does not have a clear busy and slow season, then you may consider offering the discount for midweek stays or stays lasting a day or two longer than your average stay length.

Airbnb Automation – Conclusion

First, create your electronic guidebook. I use Hostfully. Second, sign up for a PMS. I highly recommend Smartbnb. Third, follow the above instructions to create your messages and flow.

Following this strategy has cut down on my manual messages by 80-90%. You will still get questions from guests about things already covered in your listing, it is just part of the game. Airbnb encourages guests to message numerous hosts each trip. If you have ever been a guest before (if you have not, do it immediately), it is exciting to see all these homes available for you to rent at prices way below what a hotel would cost down the road. This, understandably, leads to many messages.

---

24   www.quora.com/What-percent-of-Airbnb-hosts-leave-reviews-for-their-guests

CHAPTER 19

Calendar Strategy for New Listings

Key Points

▶ Limit calendar availability and nightly maximum until you get three reviews.

▶ Charge 20-30% less than your competition.

▶ Offer extra services to encourage even more amazing reviews and increase the likely the guest leaves a timely review.

I believe momentum is involved in the Airbnb game. Either the reservations are coming in or they're not. It is important that you **start off your hosting properly so the reservations flow in from the beginning.** Below is a long-term strategy ideal for listings with 6+ months of availability. If you only rent your place out once or twice per year, this is not relevant to you.

The goal is to get three glowing positive reviews from your first three guests. Once you earn your third review, the green stars representing your overall rating start showing in the Airbnb search results.

PRIVATE ROOM · 1 BED
Perfect for Travel Nurses ..
$37 per night
2 reviews

PRIVATE ROOM · 1 BED
Private guesthouse in perfect East Sac location.

★★★★★ 21 · Superhost

"[Guests] are willing to pay a premium for places with many reviews." That quote is from Dan Hill, Director of Guest Experience at Airbnb[25]. Let's get you those first three reviews as soon as possible.

At this point, there's no need to connect to either a pricing partner or message automation. But, an electronic guidebook is needed for an optimal guest experience.

First, you will select a calendar availability of 'unavailable by default'. Second, you will set a minimum stay of one night and a maximum stay of five nights. You want to get these three reviews as quickly as possible so you can open up more calendar dates. The last thing you want is a two-week reservation during this period. Third, you will open the next three weeks for reservations. You do this because you are going to undercut your competition on price by 20-30% and you don't want a guest booking four months out at these lower prices. You undercut your competition in price to help further secure an amazing review. This could also signal to the Airbnb algorithm that you have an in-demand listing. Next time you open your calendar up, you better be high

25   spectrum.ieee.org/computing/software/the-secret-of-airbnbs-pricing-algorithm

in search so guests can find you. Furthermore, as a new host, it's likely you forgot an amenity or made some other rookie mistake. **The guest will be more lenient on you at such a discounted price.** Do not ever tell the guest they are getting your listing for a discount. It's bad form.

Limiting your calendar to get three quick, positive reviews is the crux of the strategy. You will also get an idea of what you can charge. If you got a full calendar within a half a day then you know you can up the price. Usually this strategy will take a few days to a week to fill those first three weeks. The below information can be used if you want to take it to the next level.

You can consider doing things for these first three guests that you might not otherwise do, but could result in an even more amazing review. Examples include:

- Preemptively offering luggage storage either before or after check-in.
- Offering a live check-in.
- Providing a bottle of wine as a welcome gift.
- Befriend the guests by inviting them for a drink or to share a local meal.

You may have to continue the above strategy for five to six reservations as all guests don't leave reviews and some do it towards the end of the 14-day time limit. The more extras you provide, the more likely the guest is to leave a review. **Make the guest want to share their experience at your Airbnb listing in the review!**

After you have three reviews showing in search and in your listing, you can connect to a pricing partner, open up your calendar availability, and follow the strategy as laid out in Chapter 9: Let's Talk About Revenue Management. How much calendar availability you open up depends on your location and the season. The specifics are covered in a few areas throughout the book.

CHAPTER 20

Improve Your Airbnb Profile for More Guests

Key Points

▶ A completed profile is important to guests evaluating the host for trustworthiness with leads to bookings.

▶ Add a description to your profile of about 75 words and cover a variety of topics including origin, personality, education, and interests.

The following is a summary, attributable to Peter Kwan, Co-chair of the Home Sharers Democratic Club[26], of a study on perceived trustworthiness of an Airbnb profile and the associated host choice.

Summary: A strong Airbnb profile is around 55-72 words in length and covers a diverse range of topics including interests and tastes, work or education, personality, relationships, origin or residence, travel, and hospitality.

Improve your listing performance by improving your Airbnb profile. In a recent Stanford and Cornell Tech research paper, "Self-Disclosure and Perceived Trustworthiness of Airbnb Host Profiles"[27], the researchers concluded the following:

---

26 www.homesharersdemclub.org
27 goo.gl/HPzKCA

1. How a host describes herself in her profile reduces uncertainty and signals to the guest whether the host is trustworthy. Trust is tied to ratings and reputation, although one study suggests that since Airbnb ratings are skewed high: "the number of reviews received is predictive of room sales even when controlling for scores." Another study showed that "profile images were linked to perceived trustworthiness of hosts and higher prices."

• • •

A strong Airbnb profile is around 55-72 words in length and covers a diverse range of topics including interests and tastes, work or education, personality, relationships, origin or residence, travel, and hospitality.

• • •

2. The researchers suggest a "Profile as Promise" approach "for understanding how hosts and guests produce and evaluate disclosures in Airbnb profiles. Hosts disclosed information about themselves that they perceived as relevant and of interest to potential guests, and their promises were evaluated based on their trustworthiness, as predicted by signaling theory and URT." (uncertainty reduction theory).

3. The research showed **on-site hosts had longer profiles than off-site hosts,** and are more likely to write on topics related to personality and tastes, and less likely to write about origin and residence. This helps guests to reduce the uncertainty factor when deciding to book a place where the host is also present. There is a clear relationship between longer profiles and perceived trustworthiness scores but with diminishing returns with longer profiles (increasing the mean word count from 6 to 13 increased trustworthiness scores by 18.9%, but an increase from 106 to 188 only increased trustworthiness by 2.5%).

4. Researchers also looked into the variety of topic choice on trustworthiness disclosed in the host profiles, and separated

them into: Origin or Residence, Work or Education, Interests & Tastes, and Hospitality. The study showed that as the number of topics increased in a profile, so did the trustworthiness of the profile. The most successful three-topic combination was profiles that contained topics related to Hospitality, Origin or Residence, and Work or Education.

5. Finally, the "so what?" question: does a higher trustworthiness score for text-based host profiles predict the likelihood of guest choice? The study concluded: "when profiles are short, perceived trustworthiness almost perfectly predicts choice, whereas when the profile length increases, other factors appear to influence choice. This may suggest a nuanced role of trust in decision making – there is a threshold that is needed to pass muster, but other factors ... may weigh in once trustworthiness is no longer an issue."

Additional noteworthy quotes from the study

- "On-site hosts cover more topics and write more overall."
- "On-site hosts (Median=66.12, Standard Deviation=59.66) on average wrote longer profiles (measured by word count) compared to remote hosts (M=55.85, SD=52.09)"
- **"Superhosts wrote significantly longer profiles (a mean of 72.13 words compared to 57.74 words for non-superhosts)."**
- "Quantity and diversity of information increases the perception of trust."
- "Perceived trustworthiness increases with profile length."
- "Perceived trustworthiness score is a significant predictor of host choice—especially for shorter profiles that show more variation."

CHAPTER 21

How to Complete 100% of Your Host Profile

Key Points

- ▶ Many guests read the host profile, especially when they've narrowed down to a few remaining choices.
- ▶ Try to seem similar to your guest (people like people who remind them of themselves).
- ▶ Sell yourself! Talk about the experience you delivery and mention any additional services you offer.

Of the 500+ listing optimizations I have completed, there have been only two hosts who have completed 100% of their profile. For those who do not, my guess is they do not think it is an important factor. And, they would be right. However, this thinking will get you into trouble when you start leaving multiple "unimportant" things incomplete. And, the Airbnb host profile may be more important than you think. It's low hanging fruit, so optimize it.

The Airbnb rank algorithm is complex and barely anyone knows it fully. No one can say for sure, doing X will yield Y in search. And Airbnb's algorithm will increasingly change based on the guest as Airbnb moves towards artificial intelligence. But, if there is one thing I know for sure, it is this: **Completing your Airbnb host profile to 100% will definitely not hurt you and will probably help your search, at least a little.**

PRO TIP: Enter your work email address at the bottom of the 'Edit Profile' section to earn a $30 credit.

Business Travel

Work Email Address

Add your work email and get a **$30 credit** after taking your first business trip of $75 or more.

There are 13 sections to your host profile. In order of importance:

Verify Your Offline ID

Verify your offline ID at ***www.Airbnb.com/Verify***. It gives the guest a sense of safety prior to booking and may increase your rank in search. About 40% of bookings are from guests who have never used Airbnb[28] so help them out by adding some trust to the transaction. You can also find it under 'Trust and Verification' in the 'Profile' section:

Edit Profile

Photos, Symbol, and Video

Trust and Verification

Reviews

References

Verify Your ID

Getting your Verified ID is the easiest way to help build trust in the Airbnb community. We'll verify you by matching information from an online account to an official ID. Learn more

Or, you can choose to only add the verifications you want below.

[Verify Me]

Once completed, you will see the below logo on your profile:

If you do not verify yourself, you cannot require guests to verify themselves before booking with you. You can find this setting under 'Reservation Requirements' in the 'Listings' section.

---

28   blog.atairbnb.com/guest-onboarding

Your Listings

Your Reservations

Reservation Requirements

Listings page

Identity

Your guests will need to verify their ID before booking with you. Learn More

☐ Require guests to go through verification

Save Reservation Requirements

Sell Yourself!

Tell your guests who you are. Find it at Profile > Edit Profile > Describe Yourself.

According to a *study of Airbnb host profiles* and trustworthiness in relation to host choice, Superhosts have a mean word count of 73 and address numerous topics. Refer to Chapter 20: Improve Your Airbnb Profile For More Guests for a summary of the study.

People like people who remind them of themselves. Keep that in mind when filling in your host profile (i.e, if the majority of your guests come from Australia, list Australia as your favorite destination). Additionally, you can list any extra services you offer here (refer to Chapter 35: Additional Revenue Streams).

Here is an example of a standard profile description:

I've lived here all my life and I love Airbnb which means you'll get high service and quality, local recommendations.

Feel free to book or message me first, I'm happy to answer any specific questions in advance.

By day, I am a [job].

By night, I [hobbies].

I am a well-traveled Airbnb guest. I know what a host should do to create a comfortable guest experience.

My favorite countries visited: [country 1, country 2, country 3]

Be sure to ask me about [activity one] or [activity two]. I have a special deal with the owner! I also offer airport transfer services, cooking classes, laundry service, and car rentals.

Profile Image

Make your photo a clear image of you. A family photo is okay as long as it is clear. A grainy photo looks unprofessional. Remember, your host profile is selling yourself as a host. A photo of the sunset or of your listing just doesn't seem right. It shows you put zero effort into finding a photo of yourself for the guest. An image of your company logo is okay as long as it's professional and you want to communicate a hotel-like experience. Some guests, do not want this experience so I still prefer companies put an image of their team up.

When I was running an Airbnb property management company in San Francisco a few years ago, a host was using a strategy that I hadn't thought of up until then and it's still stuck with me. His host profile was of an attractive female and so I was expecting to greet this attractive female when I went for the initial home inspection prior to managing it. Instead, a male came to the door and identified himself as the host. After some confusion, he told me that he has put up a generic attractive female image as his host profile photo as he believed that he received more reservations. This seems plausible to me. I assume some females would prefer to stay with a female, females are generally considered to be cleaner than males, and I'm sure some males prefer to book from a female host, especially an attractive one. This host never met any of the guests in person so there would never be any confusion as I had experienced. I have no data to back this up, but I find it odd that according to Airbnb, most hosts are female, but in my experience, I've met many more male hosts.

• • •

Your host profile is selling yourself as a host.

• • •

Request a Reference

Request a reference or two from a friend. This is especially important if you're a new host. If you are an established host, this is low priority, but it can only help with your credibility.

> **PRO TIP:** Request a reference at www.airbnb.com/users/references

Edit Profile

Photos, Symbol, and Video

Trust and Verification

Reviews

References

View Profile

Complete the 'About Me' Section

Complete the entire 'About Me' section. Find it at Profile > Edit Profile > School/Work/Languages.

School	
Work	e.g. Airbnb / Apple / Taco Stand
Time Zone	(GMT-08:00) Pacific Time (US & Canada)
	Your home time zone.
Languages	None
	+ Add More
	Add any languages that others can use to speak with you on Airbnb

Further Verify Yourself

Add as many verifications as you can. In your dashboard, click 'Profile', then 'Trust and Verification'. Usually you can verify email, LinkedIn, Facebook, Google, and/or American Express. In regards to linking your social media account, you are not only creating credibility, but also marketing the Airbnb platform. You can imagine Airbnb loves the free marketing and will reward you accordingly.

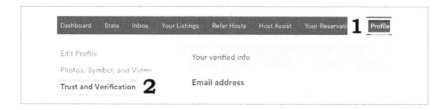

Fill In Your City

Let guests know what city you're from. Find it at Profile > Edit Profile > Where You Live. It is one small piece to the puzzle which increases guest's confidence in you are as a worthy host. And, it's so simple.

Create A Visible Wishlist

Create at least one public wish list with a few listings on it. You can view your wish lists here: https://www.airbnb.com/users/[host profile number found in URL]/wishlists or by clicking 'Saved' in the navigation bar at top.

CHAPTER 22

What to Do When a Guest Asks to Book Offline

Key Points

▶ Politely decline and state yourself (not the guest) as being the reason why.

▶ If the guest gave you a good experience, offer a small discount to book online (two for one positive reviews!).

▶ For 2+ month long reservations, it may make sense to book offline, but only if you have vacation rental insurance.

Guests asking to book offline happens all too often and all too often hosts get themselves in trouble by doing the wrong thing. A guest has a lot more upside to book offline than the host does. What should you do when you are inevitably asked to accept cash?

Politely decline.

I hope this is obvious, but do not mention anything about the guest being untrustworthy as to the reason why you do not want to book offline. Instead, **blame yourself:**

- It is for your tax and personal records at end of year.
- To keep your calendar up to date.
- For the Airbnb review.
- To get Superhost status.
- You split revenue with your housemates and need a paper trail.

- You have a process you need to follow.

I have personally hosted 250+ guests and over 1000+ reservations as an Airbnb host and property manager and have been asked about a dozen times. That is about once every 100 reservations. It is uncommon, but you should be prepared for it. **Most guests do not have bad intentions and simply want to save** the 12% (and in some cities, an extra 20-25% when Airbnb collects taxes). As a host, it never makes sense because you would only be saving 3%.

I could see an argument for actually increasing your price to earn an extra ~10% or so (you save 3% host fee, plus charge the guest an extra ~7% on the nightly rate instead of the 12-25% fee they otherwise would have paid). Still, I do not think it makes sense because you would forfeit the Airbnb Host Guarantee[29] and the Host Protection Insurance[30] on that booking. These two insurances are often confused so be sure to learn about their differences in Chapter 37: Airbnb Host Insurance Information.

Your response will differ depending on when a guest asks you to book offline: prior to booking or after they arrive.

When a Guest Asks to Book Offline Before Booking Online

If a FPG asks you through Airbnb, prior to booking, **you should 100% say no because there would be an electronic trail on this transaction**. It is also incredibly hard to communicate your personal contact info through Airbnb to the guest prior to a booking. Likely, Airbnb would flag the conversation, the guest, and you (the host) based on trigger words in the message thread. This is all bad.

Here is how I handled a recent situation. The guest put some pressure on me by making me think that I may lose the reservation because he was driving up and wanted to book immediately. He ended up booking online, but even if I lost this one, I would not have thought twice about the next time because this means the guest is only going to book offline. Why? Probably not because they want to treat your house with the utmost respect.

---

29 www.airbnb.com.au/help/article/279/what-is-the-airbnb-host-guarantee
30 www.airbnb.com.au/host-protection-insurance

It looks like you're already verified to me so they're putting you through another level. What did you do :)

Last Thursday at 09:56

No, sorry

Last Thursday at 09:56

 It is not letting me book it says it wants me to verify my identity with my statement is there anyway I can pay you cash it's not me it's Airbnb

Last Thursday at 09:47 · Vinny

Sent!

Last Thursday at 09:29

 I am on my way driving up from LA and I would like to book this before I leave so I know I am reserved

Last Thursday at 09:11 · Vinny

I still see the same price did you change it ?

Last Thursday at 09:02 · Vinny

When a Guest Asks to Book Offline After They Check-In

Let's say the guest books one night and then decides to ask you after you have met. Keep in mind, most guests are a bit cautious in asking and when you say no, they will not push it and might even apologize for asking. Most do not have any bad intentions. To be clear, I recommend you politely decline. **If the guest has proven to be a good one, I may extend them a small discount if they would like to stay additional nights. This does wonders for your reviews (two-for-one).**

Another reason to decline is that you may forget to update your calendar and create a double booking. This is especially true if you list on multiple services. If you end up having to cancel the reservation, there goes your Superhost status for 12 months and you can expect an immediate drop in search results (speaking from personal experience).

When Is It Ok To Book Offline?

Note: It is against Airbnb's terms of service to accept a payment offline that originated from Airbnb.com. Doing this could get your account cancelled.

Some people will question the above reasoning because you can earn more money by accepting reservations offline. If the guest is not paying 12%+ to Airbnb, that means more money for the host! The unscrupulous Airbnb host will cite tax savings as to why you should accept offline bookings.

If you are to accept bookings offline, then you should have your own personal brand and website (Lodgify (www.lodgify.com/#_1_b3) has made this process very easy for the person of average technical abilities). You should also have a solid short-term rental insurance policy that covers both theft, personal injury, and damage to the property including extreme situations like a fire. This makes sense if you are running a professional Airbnb property management business.

> PRO TIP: Sometimes guests want to see the place before they book, especially if the reservation is for 1+ month. I think this makes sense. To get around the system, you can agree to meet at a local store nearby the listing. If the booking originated from Airbnb, you should ask the guest to book through Airbnb.

CHAPTER 23

Why You Should Only List on One Vacation Rental Platform

Key Points

► Focusing your reviews on one platform is a great long-term ranking strategy.

► Much time is needed to maintain an optimized listing on numerous platforms.

► It may make sense to list on a 2nd platform if it allows you to only accept reservations within 2-4 weeks.

► Consider listing on Peerspace (prsp.ac/2udGTtn), the Airbnb of professional event rentals.

"We publish your listing on the top 50 platforms!"

"Vacation rental management...across hundreds of sites."

"Maximize your revenue! We create your listing on the leading 6+ platforms."

Have you seen these before? You are at least familiar with the marketing jargon. It is commonplace that to be a successful vacation rental host, you need to be listed on as many platforms as possible. The more the merrier! I have an alternate perspective for you.

Here's why, if at all possible, you do not want to list on multiple vacation rental platforms:

1. You distribute all your reviews to many platforms instead of focusing them on one.
2. You create mediocre listings on many platforms instead of one optimized listing.

Obviously, reviews are tremendously important to your search rank. The more positive reviews you have, the higher you rank. Plain and simple (see below for direct evidence). **When you list on multiple platforms, you are distributing your hard-earned reviews** instead of focusing them onto one. While this may be a good short-term strategy, it is a bad long-term strategy.

Listing on multiple vacation rental platforms is a good short-term strategy where you will surely fill in a few otherwise un-booked gaps. But this advantage quickly disappears as time goes on when having more reviews associated to your listing disproportionality affects your search rank. In other words, the listing which specialized in one platform quickly has many more reviews than the listing on numerous platforms.

Here's a graphic from EverBook's Pro service (www.everbooked.com) showing the number of reviews for Airbnb listings in Las Vegas (top) and Los Angeles (bottom). You can see there is less competition at the top. If you create your Airbnb listing today, you will be playing catch up.

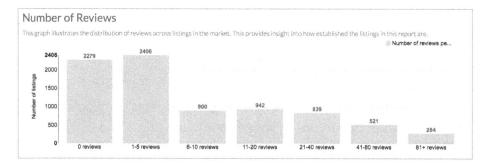

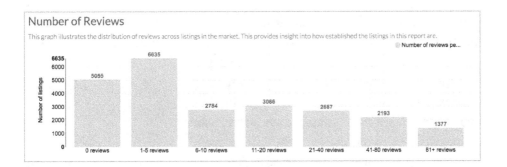

In early 2017 some research was done on Airbnb search and posted to Reddit[31]. It shows that both guest satisfaction (#1) and number of reviews (#9) are highly correlated with search ranking. Read the full report on hacking Airbnb's search rank algorithm[32].

Rank	Factor	Correlation to Page Rank
1	Guest Satisfaction	0.906
2	Absolute Price	0.901
3	Listing Word Count	0.897
4	Minimum Stay Length	0.885
5	Days since calendar updated	0.884
6	Price/Bed	0.869
7	Description Length	0.867
8	Is Instant Book	0.844
9	Review Count	0.828
10	Saved to Wishlist	0.819
11	# of Amenities	0.793
12	# of Pictures	0.785
13	Is SuperHost	0.783
14	Response Speed	0.765
15	Guest Capactiy	0.756
16	Hosted by Business	0.690
17	Is Business Ready	0.612
18	# of Other Properties Hosted	0.606
19	# of Beds	0.479
20	Cancellation Policy	0.379
21	Male-to-Female Ratio	0.357
22	Has Pets on Property	0.232
23	Beds per Guest	0.189
24	Account Age	0.119
25	Allows Smoking	0.087
26	"suburb name" in Description	0.047
27	"view" in Description	0.044

Figure 12: Correlation to search rank

---

31   goo.gl/loa467
32   goo.gl/xWcgOF

If you use multiple vacation rental platforms, only allow secondary platforms to make reservations in the next 15 to 30 days.

The above tip is the only reason I can argue for in favor of listing on multiple vacation rental platforms. That is, to use additional platforms to fill in available days within the next two weeks to one month. The average Airbnb guest books 30 days in advance making the likelihood of getting a reservation within 30 days less and less likely as the unbooked days approach. As we all know, these last-minute bookings also pose the greatest risk. Scammers and thieves are not planning ahead 30 days in advance.

> • • •
>
> Only use additional platforms to fill in available days within the next two weeks to one month.
>
> • • •

Additionally, you may have started with an optimized listing on those 10 websites, but **after a year they are all now poorly optimized** because you have not kept up with the constant changes and updates these platforms make on a monthly basis.

One final thought...

Have you heard of the Pareto principle? Or the 80/20 rule? It says that 20% of your efforts result in 80% of your outcomes. For Airbnb property managers, 20% of your Airbnb listings result in 80% of your income.

This is true in society: 80% of land is owned by 20% of the population.

Also true in nature: 20% of a crop creates 80% of the yield.

In my experience, Airbnb generates ~70-80% of booking revenue in most markets. A good host with an optimized listing can get this number up to 90%+.

If you are saying to yourself you want that extra 10-20%, I would ask: **Is the extra 20% profit worth the extra 80% of your time?** Time is your only asset you will never get back. Money comes and goes. For me, I would rather focus my attention on the most popular website, Airbnb.com, and use the rest of my time with family or friends or on hobbies or (ready for it!) to **create an additional stream of revenue** than chasing the last bit of income from the 5th most popular vacation rental platform.

With that said, it may make sense to **list on multiple platforms if, for some reason, Airbnb is not the market leader in your area**. Areas in China immediately come to mind or areas with a very specific clientele who already have a process for booking their vacation rentals.

PART IV

Company +
Book Reviews

There are an amazing number of companies
providing various service to Airbnb hosts.

Visit the recommended companies section
at www.OptimizeYOURAirbnb.com to see
a full list organized by category.

CHAPTER 24

Smartbnb Review + Guide, Message Automation

Key Points

▶ Smartbnb automates much of your Airbnb from initial inquiry to guest review.

▶ Automates communication with cleaning and check-in teams.

▶ Many additional features like Market Report, Heartbeats, Stealth Mode, and Checkpoint explained.

▶ See Chapter 18: Optimizing and Automating Your Messages on how to optimize your Smartbnb messages.

This Smartbnb review is perfect for the Airbnb host who only, or mostly, uses Airbnb. I have been using Smartbnb for one year and it offers almost all the functionality of Guesty, the market leader, for a fraction of the cost. Plus, the founder, Pierre-Camille Hamana, responds to some of the customer service chats that come in. Currently, Smartbnb is only compatible with Airbnb (though, I hear this will change).

It is always daunting to learn a new piece of software, but this chapter will provide you a perfect overview so you can master it in half the time. You may also watch the video on my YouTube channel. If you are already familiar with similar software (Porter, AirGMS, Guesty, etc.) this chapter will highlight the differences unique to Smartbnb. One thing to note immediately is upon account creation, templates are already setup and turned on for you in the Messaging component (i.e. the meat and potatoes component). This saves you time, but beware these message go out to guests as soon as you signup.

There are a few unique features to Smartbnb:

Heartbeats – Smartbnb will send Airbnb a signal letting them know your calendar is up to date. Your listing will always appear to guests as having been recently updated. Having an up to date calendar positively affects your search rank.

Market – Sends you a daily report letting you know where your listing ranks based on your city, number of guests, and listing type. Here's an article on how to read this report: https://goo.gl/s2cLPF.

> • • •
>
> Upon account creation, templates are already set up and turned on .
>
> • • •

Stealth – If you would like to unlist during certain hours of the day/days of the week, this feature automates that process for you while allowing you to remain listed on the weekends, if you choose. If this feature does not make sense to you, it is a good thing.

Checkpoint – This functionality is only applicable if you require FPGs to verify their ID before booking with you.

It fixes a loophole of Airbnb which does not notify the host when a guest has paid for a booking but has not verified their profile. The reservation is not presented to the host until the guest verification is completed. If the host is not informed, they cannot help guide the guest through the verification process, but the calendar is blocked for up to 12 hours. However, this has been known to not function properly and I recently had to call Airbnb to get them to manually remove the reservation as it was on my calendar blocking days for over 24 hours. Needless to say, this feature is powerful. It notifies the host of the booking and starts a conversation with the guest to help them complete the verification. As always, this can be fully automated.

Smartbnb Messaging

This is the 'meat and potatoes' component and where you will spend 85% of your time. It has five message flows that I will explain here.

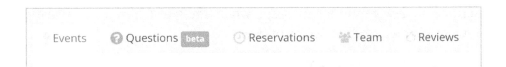

Smartbnb Messaging – Events

The events message flow relates to new inquiries, pre-approvals, requests to book, accepted reservations, cancelled reservations, and a few other less used 'events'.

I use it for inquiries, requests to book, reservations, and pre-approvals. It comes pre-populated with templates you can alter for your needs or delete.

Note: When adding any additional messages, a template is not populated.

You are able to tell Smartbnb to automatically pre-approve all inquiries in this section.

Smartbnb supports 29 languages and allows you to create a template in any of them. The software automatically detects the preferred language of the guest and sends the appropriate template.

Smartbnb Messaging – Questions

The question flow is Smartbnb's beta test with artificial intelligence. Based on answers you prepare to common guest questions (parking, discounts, etc.), the software will edit your message templates to include those answers only when a guest asks.

This is a promising area for development, but I suggest skipping this section until the kinks are worked out unless you have many listings and find yourself repeatedly answering the same questions. You can setup responses here for guests asking questions related to discounts, parking, Wi-Fi, infants, and pets.

Smartbnb Messaging – Reservations

The reservation message flow communicates with the guest before, during, and after a reservation. This means when creating templates, you will send it based on check-in or check-out time. You can also setup a review reminder message when the guest has yet to leave a review after a certain amount of days.

Smartbnb Messaging – Team

This message flow is meant for service providers, namely cleaners or check-in people. I send a message to my cleaners whenever a reservation is confirmed, altered, or canceled. First, you add your service provider. Then, you create the message and define when it will be sent.

Smartbnb Messaging – Reviews

Smartbnb will automatically review your guests based on a pre-loaded template you can edit. You are allowed to add many review templates and customize each by adding the guest's name. You also specify when the review is to be posted.

If you want to leave the guest a negative review, you will need to remember to log in to Smartbnb and edit the review related to the particular guest before the system auto-posts it. You can also activate a 'bad' review mode which delays the posting until the last moment. As you can imagine, this feature is awesome!

Smartbnb Support

You know how frustrating it is to call customer service only to know more than them? Camille Hamana personally responds to some of your chat requests. I love this feature because there were a few times during setup and then ongoing for the first few weeks where I had a question before I could continue. Camille Hamana or the knowledgeable customer service team often responded right away, but no less than a few hours later no matter the time of day. Look for the live chat icon in the lower-right area.

Why I Love and Recommend Smartbnb

The software is **exclusive to Airbnb**. It tells me that Camille Hamana is focusing all his energy on one system rather than trying to integrate with all (and probably being mediocre on all). I assume this will eventually change, but he has taken his time to perfect Airbnb first. It is evident from using his software and seeing the constant improvements that he is the real deal.

The **system is 90% setup for you right when you sign up**. After all, those who want automation may not have the time to automate. The messages alone save you a couple hours of time. However, everything is turned on upon signup so beware. Also, your email box will be flooded with new messages as Smartbnb emails you with all actions taken. You'll want to setup a filter for Smartbnb emails as there is no way to turn them off.

Pricing is fixed instead of percentage based like the competition. Regardless if a reservation is for $100 or $1000, the software does no additional work so I should not pay additionally for a higher reservation. In my experience, this makes Smartbnb about 70% **cheaper than the competition**.

I love the chat box, especially during setup when it can be frustrating to learn new software. Having Camille Hamana, the man who created every line of code, answer your chats is icing on the cake.

Smartbnb Review – Other Notes

Create a new email address to use with Smartbnb and Airbnb. The emails will automatically forward to an account of your choosing. This is most useful for Airbnb property managers.

Connect with MailChimp to automatically add prior guests to an email list. As Airbnb uses reservation specific emails, Smartbnb has designed a process to message the guest asking for their real email which is then added to MailChimp. This is all automatic. You can then target your prior guests with future deals.

You can simulate any message template within the 'edit' message page to see how a live message would look to a guest. So don't worry if you're not sure about a short code usage, you can test it here.

If you are using booking platforms in addition to Airbnb, you can consider the following companies which have integrations with many platforms. I have tested and used all of these recommendatios:

- Porter (www.yourporter.com) – Integrates with HomeAway, TripAdvisor, Wimdu, and Booking.com. Use OPTIMIZE for $20 off your first month plus a 21-day free trial. First listing is free.
- AirGMS (www.airgms.com) – Designed for Airbnb, but you can integrate other third-party calendars. First listing is free.
- Guesty (www.guesty.com) – Market leader with a ton of additional functionality, though, they are the most expensive at 2-5% of each booking.

CHAPTER 25

PriceLabs, Smart Pricing Tool

Key Points

▶ Using an intelligent pricing tool is a must. I use PriceLabs, but there are two viable alternatives, Beyong Pricing and Wheelhouse.

▶ None of these tools are set-it-and-forget-it, you still must monitor them monthly.

▶ Provides numerous functionality that Airbnb's Smart Pricing does not.

▶ Remember, 'base price' is what you would charge on an average night in an average month.

▶ Readers get a 30-day free trial plus 50% off your first bill.

Introduction

I use PriceLabs for all of my Airbnb activity whether the listing is my own, one I manage revenue for, or one I am the property manager. I routinely monitor and test many companies in the smart pricing niche, including Airbnb's Smart Pricing functionality.

The Airbnb smart pricing arena is competitive with many quality companies (Wheelhouse and Beyond Pricing being the two main competitors). I will explain why I prefer PriceLabs below.

If you are thinking, "What the heck is a smart pricing company?", let me explain. A smart pricing (or intelligent pricing) company updates your Airbnb calendar daily with nightly rates depending on many variables. After you initially setup the system, it's automated. Here is a nice graphic from the PriceLabs site that pictorially explains what intelligent pricing software does:

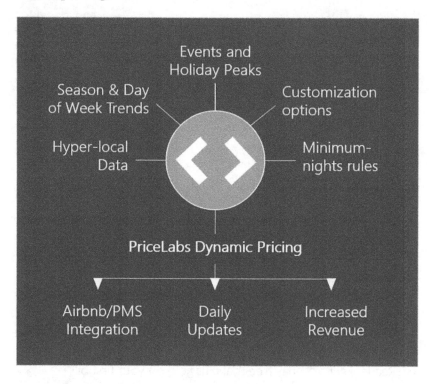

Overall Recommendation + Why

Overall Score – 9/10

Cost – PriceLabs charges a flat fee rather than a percentage. For U.S, Canada, and European countries, the price is $20 for the first listing and goes down to $5 for the 100th (other countries pay less). I prefer this because whether my reservation is for $100 or $1000, the software is doing the same amount of work. PriceLabs will be the cheapest option for anyone with 70%+ occupancy and a daily rate of about $75 or more.

Daily Rates – PriceLabs varies the daily prices more than the others. You may or may not prefer this. I prefer it. The nearer unbooked dates go lower and the further out unbooked dates go high (typically) than the other services. This is important if you want to maximize your revenue as you'll undercut your competition and charge more during optimal times.

Customization – The customization functionality is impressive and probably pays back the monthly fee. However, you need to set time aside to learn the intricacies. This chapter will go over how to use the most popular functionality. Refer to my detailed blog post for all else[33].

Customer Support – Email only, however, I have found the wait time is minimal. As far as I can remember they have responded same day within a few hours every time I have had to send an email over the past year I've been using the service.

The 'Review Prices' Dashboard

The PriceLabs 'Review Prices' dashboard is what you see upon sig-nin and is mostly straightforward. The less straightforward columns are:

Customization Group – Allows you to apply standard customizations to a group of listings rather than applying and changing them individually. PriceLabs has written a lengthier version of this feature (blog.pricelabs.co/customization-groups).

Tags – Allows for better sorting. For example, if you have listings in different cities, you can identify them here.

Base – **Your base price is what you would expect on an average night in an average month.** Either go with PriceLabs suggested base price (which is usually pretty accurate) or take a guess. Regardless, you

33   optimizemyairbnb.com/pricelabs-review-airbnb-smart-pricing

will have to monitor and adjust your base price throughout the year as booking trends change.

Let's take a quick break from this PriceLabs review for an important public service announcement on a common question I get asked: **What should my base price be?**

If you are not sure what this number might be, PriceLabs recommends a base price and they provide you with some information if you click on 'Base Price Help' within the listing calendar.

However, do not spend more than two minutes deciding your base price because you are going to have to adjust it. These smart pricing tools are not a set-it-and-forget-it software. You will have to monitor, at least monthly. If you place your base price at X and the next two months are booked at 100% occupancy within a week then you priced it too low and should raise your base price X+10%. Alternatively, most Airbnb hosts overvalue their space. If you have a low occupancy rate and are barely getting inquiries, then decrease your base price 10%. Refer to Chapter 9: Let's Talk About Revenue Management to read about my revenue maximization strategy.

Ok. Back to the Review and the 'Review Prices' dashboard...

7/30/60 day – Represents percentage of days *open* in the next 7, 30, and 60 days, respectively. The other services show the percentage of days booked so this is something you will have to adjust to had you been using a different service. High numbers bad, low numbers good.

Review Prices – This green button is where the magic happens and takes you to each individual Airbnb calendar where you have more customizations available to you.

The Listing Calendar Dashboard

This is where you come after you click the green 'Review Prices' button to the right of every row on the main dashboard. You will see a lot of the same information as the account dashboard with two very large distinctions: 'Customizations' and 'Recommended & Custom Pricing Calendar'.

Note: If you make any changes to the 'Lowest', 'Base', or 'Highest' boxes you need to click 'Save/Refresh'. If you make changes to the calendar directly, like changing a daily price, you do not need to click 'Save/Refresh' unless you want the change to take effect immediately (instead of over night).

The 'Sync Now' button will update your prices in Airbnb within a few minutes. We will explore the 'Customizations' section in detail below. Any customization you create will override the existing price.

Customizations – Last Minute Prices

A common complaint of an Airbnb host using Airbnb's Smart Pricing or other third-party pricing tools is that they do not have enough control over last minute discounts. PriceLabs fixed this. You have three options: Fixed, % – Flat, or % – Gradual. The main difference is whether the system applies a fixed daily rate to a certain number of days or a percentage discount.

Customizations – Orphan Day Prices

This feature is super neat! I am not sure why Airbnb has never figured this out for themselves as it would make both the host and Airbnb more money plus increase the number of available days for the guest. That is the definition of a win-win-win.

An orphan night is defined as a night that cannot be booked due to your minimum nights requirements. For example, if you have a three-day minimum and a gap of two nights on your calendar, that two-night gap cannot be booked (i.e. an orphan night). This customization is meant for Airbnb hosts with a two-night minimum or higher and is to be used in conjunction with the minimum stay customization discussed one section below. This customization will allow you to raise or lower the suggested daily rate for any orphan nights.

I recommend an increase for orphan nights to avoid guests who are interested in getting a single-night deal for a party. Additionally, orphan nights can be a month or more into the future and there is no reason to discount that far in advance.

Customizations – Minimum Stay Update

This setting allows you to book otherwise orphan nights. It is a bit complicated but powerful. PriceLabs has written a detailed explanation of their minimum night customizations[34] for your viewing pleasure.

Important note: **if you change any of these settings, PriceLabs will overwrite any existing settings in your Airbnb account related to minimum nights**.

You must first switch ON the 'Minimum Stay Update' customization and three more options will appear below (as covered in the next three sections).

Fixed – There are three options, but you will probably use this option. The first box represents your general minimum (in number of days) to be applied to all days. The second box (ie on the right side) represents a minimum you want to set on the weekends. A weekend is defined as either a Friday or Saturday in the reservation. For example, if you require a 3-night minimum on weekends, this could include any combination of the following reservations: W/Th/Fri, Th/Fi/Sa, Fr/Sa/Su, or Sa/Su/Mo.

Minimum Stay For Last Minute Bookings

This customization changes your minimum stay requirements for near un-booked days (i.e. Change my minimum to one night if un-booked nights exist within three days from today).

BEWARE! If you do this, depending on your area and your listing settings, you might want to raise the price of this vacancy. A last-minute

34 blog.pricelabs.co/minimum-night-settings

reservation is higher risk than one made in advance. Think about it, most partiers and thieves are not planning 30 days in advance.

Minimum Stay For Far Out Bookings

Allows you to increase your minimum night requirement on any reservation further than X days. I am torn on this one. On one hand, it seems to make sense to try and get more days per reservation if that reservation is far out into the future (at least 90 days). On the other hand, if you are getting a good rate as you will with PriceLabs (the further out the booking, the higher the price), then you may miss out on a premium priced reservation because you want an extra night on that reservation. Additionally, if that reservation comes during slow season, I think we all would be happy to accept it well in advance. Side note: **Be wary of guests booking too far in advance as they may know something you do not leading to an unfairly priced reservation.**

Minimum Stay For Orphan Bookings

This is so cool! Likely, you will use this in conjunction with the 'Orphan Day Prices' customization above.

Length of gap – This allows for a dynamic minimum night requirement depending on the length of the gap. For example, the screenshot below tells the system to make the minimum night requirement equal to the gap of un-booked days as long as the gap is either one or two nights. This would be a suitable setting for an Airbnb listing with a three-night minimum (i.e. potential for 1 and 2 orphan night days between bookings).

Minimum Stay for Orphan Bookings						ON
Length of gap ⬍	day(s) minimum for gaps between	1	⬍	and	2	⬍

Customizations Dashboard

Dynamic Pricing ▾	Market Intelligence	Account new! ▾
Review Prices		
Manage Listings		
Customizations		

This is an advanced section. PriceLabs allows you to create customizations that apply to your entire account, a group of listings that you setup, or individual listings. This creates a hierarchy problem where you have more than one customization on the same listing. Luckily, PriceLabs has explained their hierarchy rules[35].

Account Level Customizations – You can create any of the customizations we talked about above once and apply them to all of your listings with this feature.

Group Customizations – If you have two or more distinct groups of Airbnb listings where an entire account customization would not work, then you will want to create a group. This would be used in any case where you want to apply different customizations to different listings for any reason.

Listing level customizations – This is your one-stop shop to adjust any customization on any specific listing rather than having to first click the 'Review Prices' button on the main dashboard for each listing you want to edit.

Manage Listings Dashboard

This looks a lot like the PriceLabs 'Review Prices' Dashboard...and it is very similar. Here are the differences:

PMS – Lets you know which vacation rental system the listing is connected to. They list Airbnb as a PMS which it is not (it's a vacation rental platform like VRBO), but it still will be found in this section as it is treated the same.

Customization Group – If you created a 'Group Customization' in the 'Customization' dashboard, here is where you can group the listings associated to any group.

Show Listing – Uncheck if you want a particular listing to not appear in the 'Review Prices' dashboard

Tags – Another option to group listings as you see fit with text descriptions.

Low/Base/Highest Price – If you had pricing adjustments to make to the minimums, base, or high price on numerous listings you could do that here without having to click into each individual listing.

Map Listing – Useful for users who integrate their PMS with Price-Labs. Some PMS systems do not integrate with Airbnb, so in that case the map functionality lets PriceLabs know which PMS listing corresponds to which Airbnb listing so that 1) they can maintain price parity and 2) they do not double charge because it is the same listing just listed in multiple places. The extra channel costs one dollar per channel. **If you use a PMS, this becomes your main calendar and you should integrate your pricing through your PMS rather than the platform (ie Airbnb).**

Customer Support

PriceLabs offers email only support, but they do respond rapidly. They post their support email in numerous places so you cannot miss it. Email them at support@PriceLabs.co (not a typo, it is '.co').

Conclusion

PriceLabs is like poker. You can learn it quickly, but unlocking its full potential (customizations) takes time. Start slow. Sign up, connect your account, and input your minimum and base prices. Then, chill for a week. Then, learn one customization per week starting with the 'Last Minute Prices' customization.

I love PriceLabs because of the variety of customizations allowed, the low fixed price point, and, of course, the daily rates. I also love that it is available globally and have recommend it to many of the hosts I have worked with.

Visit PriceLabs (goo.gl/5b3BVh) to receive **50% off your first bill** plus 30 days free to try out the software.

CHAPTER 26

Payfully, Payment Advancement

Key Points

▶ Access future reservation payouts up to 90 days early for a fee of ~3-10%.

▶ You must have a verified ID account.

▶ Use OPTIMIZE for a free first advance.

Payfully enables hosts to receive funds from their future reservations in advance, for a very small fee. One of the first things you learn as a new Airbnb host when it comes to payments is that you don't get paid out until after the guest arrives (24 hours after check-in to be exact). That means a reservation in three months from today is worthless to you until the date of the reservation. This makes sense due to cancellations or alterations but is still annoying.

Have a trip coming up that you need to purchase things for now? Like flights and accommodations? Maybe a holiday is coming up where you need some extra cash to purchase gifts in advance when they're on sale? Payfully can help you solve these problems.

The service is simple and cheap. The website is clear, too. I'm going to walk you through my interaction with the service.

The two-step signup process is easy. First, create an account with your email address. The account does not have to be associated with your Airbnb account.

Second, connect your Airbnb account. I signed up with an active Airbnb host account and it took about 15 seconds to load my data.

Once complete, your dashboard is automatically populated with your future reservation data. On the left side is your Airbnb data and the right side has the amount per reservation you can be advanced. It also clearly states the associated fee and when you can expect to receive the money. The site states a $15 to $55 (3%-11%) fee per $500 advance. When I added up my total available to be advanced, I got $4,534 with fees totaling $158, or 3.5%. This seems extremely reasonable to me. All of my reservations were within 30 days. The company says they're able to advance payments up to 90 days out.

It's all very clear. You'll notice the instant message chat box to the bottom-right. Thankfully this trend is catching on and I'm a huge fan of it. No more digging around to figure out how to email for help. Reach a Payfully employee immediately with this neat feature.

I went ahead and requested an advance on one of my future reservations. You're asked to sign an online document. The document asks for your name, address, email, and signature. Your name, address, and email must match your Airbnb account. This could get tricky if you have a joint account with your spouse. It could also get tricky if your address is not entered correctly which a lot of hosts do for security reasons as Airbnb communicates the address to the guest immediately upon booking which could be a few months early. After speaking with the company, they said that if these things do not match, it will raise red flags in the system and they'll ask for additional verifications. Typically, they're able to work through issues like this, but the advance may take an extra few days to be remitted until the information is verified.

• • •

When I added up my total available to be advanced, I got $4,534 with fees totaling $158, or 3.5%.

• • •

Note: **You must have a Verified ID in Airbnb.**

Once you sign the document (be sure to confirm your signature through your email), you're taken to a screen that allows you to connect your bank account to let Payfully know where to deposit the advance. But, no more signing in online and getting your account number and trying to figure out which routing number to choose. Payfully has made this part super easy by allowing you to choose your bank, enter your login credentials, and your accounts are automatically populated. After you choose one, you confirm the details, and submit. This is also the screen where you can enter OPTIMIZE to get your first advance free.

One thing I assumed going in was that the advance would be for the total Airbnb payout, plus I would pay a fee. Instead, Payfully remits the Airbnb payout minus their fee. This actually makes more sense. If they did it using my assumption, you'd have to track the reservation and make sure you have a bit extra in your account to cover the fee. The way they do it, you can totally forget about it because the exact payout will be withdrawn having no net effect on your account.

If you request an advance, be sure to do it early in the day and **you could get the money as soon as the next business day** as long as all your documents and information is correct. Otherwise, it will take two days.

In summary, the website is extremely clear and straightforward and the process to request an advance is well thought out and easy to follow. From account creation to confirming an advance, may take you ten minutes maximum. The fees are extremely reasonable, a lot lower than my expectation going in. Be sure to use OPTIMIZE to get your first advance free[36].

An alternative to consider is Clearbanc[37]. They provide larger loans to vacation rental owners based on prior account activity and future projections. They're geared towards financing professionals who want to expand their vacation rental business rather than personal loans. I have not used their service. Clearbanc has extended a 10% discount to readers of Optimize YOUR Airbnb. To claim, go to www.OptimizeYourAirbnb.com and click 'Claim Bonus'.

---

36   https://goo.gl/9kAcq8
37   https://goo.gl/E9SGgp

CHAPTER 27

Hostfully Review, Electronic Guidebook

Key Points

- ▶ Hostfully provides software to create electronic guidebooks to send to your guest.
- ▶ Creating an electronic guidebook not only improves the guest experience, but saves you time in not having to answer standard questions.
- ▶ Refer to Chapter 30: How To Put Your Airbnb On Autopilot on how to incorporate an electronic guidebook in the reservation process.
- ▶ Use OPTIMIZE to get two-months free of Pro service.

You need an electronic guidebook. It's not optional. Unfortunately, many Airbnb hosts view guidebooks as solely a cost or a nice-to-have. Not only is it extremely useful to the guest (speaking from experience), but it'll save you countless hours in not answering the same questions over and over. It brings a professional aurora to your hosting style. To add to that, unlike many other tools

NOTE: I've recorded a YouTube video with David Jacoby, Hostfully Founder, where he gives a demo of the product and I ask questions to clarify certain points I had trouble with while using the product. The video is supplemental to this and is meant to provide a live view of the product plus sprinkle you with best practices and tips to create the best guidebook. See it here: goo.gl/Si1gxz

I recommend, this is a set-it-and-forget it tool (except for the occasional update).

If you're unfamiliar with electronic guidebooks, here's what it looks like (this is the desktop version):

Why Not Just Use Airbnb?

If the above photo doesn't do a good enough job of answering this question, let me explain...The 'House Manual' within Airbnb is not sufficient because of two main factors:

1. No organization – you are only allowed to add text so the guest will have to dig through to find the info they want.
2. Time of delivery – it is presented to the guest at time of booking. The guest does not need this info until they are near check-in. If you present it any sooner, it's information overload and the guest starts to devalue any information you send their way.

Why Hostfully?

There are many options on the market. I test all of them and my favorites are Coral and Hostfully. I am writing a review on Hostfully as they have outpaced the others in terms of innovation and progress. They're also the market leader and doing a good job at branding to try and get guests to recognize Hostfully so they know they're in good hands if the host uses them.

Before I jump into the review, I want to call out a few items:

1. Hostfully has one of the top travel blogs on Medium[38], even outranking Airbnb's Design and Engineering department. Yours truly has been featured on it a handful of times!

2. This is not an app. It's a mobile optimized webpage meaning it works equally well on computer and phone screens without having to download an app.

3. There is a useful demo guidebook on the Hostfully homepage[39]. Understand that yours won't look like this right away. You will add to it over time. Drag the browser window to the size of a smartphone to see what it will look like on mobile.

4. You can print a physical copy of the guidebook. If you do this, buy plastic covers or laminate the pages so they stay looking new.

5. Hostfully provides a badge to let guests know you are a Hostfully Host (i.e. use their guidebook). I recommend using this and adding it towards the second half of your photos as it won't make a guest book your place, but it could be one of many items that puts you over the edge.

Cost

As an individual host, **you can create and use one guidebook for free.** There are upgrades that you may want, but I find the free version is sufficient. If you have many properties, they charge starting at $7.99 per property per month. If you are a property manager or an individual with 5+ properties, they have an enterprise level package. Use OPTIMIZE for two-months free of Hostfully Pro.

---

38   travel.hostfully.com
39   v2.hostfully.com/california-dreaming

What I Like

Admittedly, this first one is a personal preference, but it made an immediate positive first impression on me. We all know how important first impressions are! When you create a login to their website, they do not require you to input your password twice. This always annoyed me on other websites as if subtlety hinting I'm incapable of entering my chosen password once correctly. As if I have to enter it a second time to protect me from myself. Anyways, it started things off on the right foot.

I love that the first guidebook is free. And, their intention is to have the first guidebooks always be free. This means that a host with a $25 per night room can be just as professional as the host with a $250 per night home. This is important to me.

Amazingly easy to add recommendations. This is a huge time saver. It's actually fun to add recommendations. Simply, type the name of the recommendation and Hostfully automatically fills in everything else including letting you choose a professional photo. They want you to make the recommendation personal and tell the guest why you're recommending it, so text is not automatically added.

> **PRO TIP:** Have your typical guest in mind when adding recommendations. A Michelin ranked restaurant for the guest renting a $50 per night Airbnb doesn't make sense.

The guidebooks are not indexed by Google so you can feel safe putting secure information in there. However, as a word of caution, I recommend you separate the address and entry info to protect yourself.

What I Don't Like

I found the process/UX of creating a guidebook to have some friction. It's not super clear what the next step is upon sign-in. Instead, you have to read a bit as they introduce unfamiliar concepts (Decks vs Cards vs. Guidebooks) right away. The above referenced YouTube video is meant to bypass this confusion. To clarify, cards are pieces of information (check-in instructions, trash info, wifi, recommendations, etc.) while decks are guidebooks. However, you'll see Hostfully refer to both Decks and Guidebooks throughout. Just know, they are used interchangeably.

> **PRO TIP:** If you attract foreigners who do not know the local language, include basic phrases with recordings from Forvo.com as a card in your guidebook.

You don't create cards then create the guidebook which is what I thought after reading about cards vs desks. Instead, you simultaneously create a guidebook with the necessary cards. To be clear, this is how I expected the process to flow so the extra verbiage (card vs deck) just added unnecessary confusion for me.

Customer Support

Hostfully is a busy, growing startup, but I've only ever experienced quick email responses. They seem to go over and above with helping you. There's no chat box on their website, something I think would be really useful for the host creating a first guidebook, but you can email them at Support@Hostfully.com.

Overall Thoughts

Hostfully will take you about 30 minutes to create your first guidebook and save you hours of future time in answering guest questions. It's clear that Hostfully is the market leader and dedicated to providing the best electronic guidebooks on the market. From their impressive blog to their useful email campaigns, Hostfully and electronic guidebooks have become synonyms in my mind.

CHAPTER 28

NoiseAware + Party Squasher Review, Noise Monitoring

Key Points

▶ NoiseAware and Party Squasher help you monitor the noise level and number of people in your Airbnb, respectively.

▶ These tools are important in pre-emptively thwarting noise violations, neighbor issues, and potential damage.

▶ Use OPTIMIZE on either site for 20% off your order.

NoiseAware and Party Squasher are smart home sensors that detect noise levels and number of wireless devices, respectively, and alert hosts when a risky situation, such as a party, is likely to be taking place.

This graphic from NoiseAware sums up what these tools are for. The chart is measuring noise being picked up by the sensor. The drop occurs after the host sent a message to the guest:

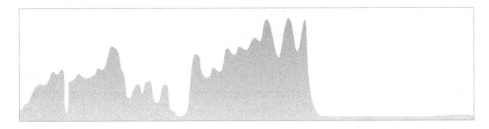

There are two questions the unfamiliar host asks:

- Will the guests steal from me?
- Will the guests throw a party in my home?

Luckily both are rare, but party-throwing guests are much more common. Even more common are the impromptu late evening gathering in the backyard. Regardless, it only takes one bad apple. A complaining neighbor can do a lot of thwart your Airbnb. Trust me, I know.

Pre NoiseAware/Party Squasher, you might drive by your place to check on it, ask neighbors to be on the lookout or notify you of anything suspicious (extra cars, loud music, etc). In one case I know a host who installed cameras on the exterior of the house.

Post NoiseAware/Party Squasher, you await an early warning alert from your phone.

When I began hosting 100% remotely, I started seriously researching noise monitoring devices and I found two noteworthy companies. NoiseAware monitors the volume of noise while Party Squasher monitors the number of devices connected to your wifi network. After doing a bit of research, including using my social network to initially vet both companies (surprisingly, I was able to find zero unhappy customers), I tried them out.

How To Use It

The sensors plug into your outlet and connect to your wifi. Set-up is a breeze. It took only about 5 minutes. Be sure to use a screw to bolt the device to the outlet faceplate so the guest won't accidentally unplug it.

For NoiseAware, once you receive an alert it's only after noise has been escalated at the property for a time span over 5 minutes. For Party Squasher, you set the number of allowable devices based on your occupancy (I set mine at 3x occupancy as I only want to know when it gets excessive).

If and when you find yourself with a situation, first send a message through the app. Nine of ten times the guest will respond within fifteen minutes. Here's an example message NoiseAware sent me which has been used successfully with their users:

> *Hello <Guest Name>, this is <Host Name>. I hope your stay is going well! I'm sending you this message to let you know that the property you are staying in has recently received a noise complaint. We take quiet hours seriously so please make sure to keep the noise at a reasonable level during your stay. We are here to make sure you have an awesome stay so please let us know if there is anything we can do for you!*

If your house ever loses power or the wifi signal, the devices will alert you and start working immediately upon power or reconnecting to wifi.

Pros

NoiseAware uses an algorithm that can distinguish a truly risky situation from merely a loud noise. It's spot on. Their sensors are incapable of recording any audio, which is a huge win in terms of privacy rights. Be sure to let the guest know if you have installed one of these monitors. Here is example text from NoiseAware:

We use smart home technology to improve your experience. NoiseAware is a smart home device that measures volume levels throughout the property, and allows us to respond to noise nuisances without disrupting your stay. NoiseAware is privacy compliant and is required on this property[40].

Party Squasher couldn't be simpler. This is truly their strong suit. Buy it, download the app, plug it in, and you're off. So simple.

Cons

While NoiseAware can detect volume, they can't give you any more information. You can view the last three hours of noise data, but its usefulness is limited. Enter, Party Squasher, who counts the number of devices. With these two pieces of hardware, you can start to get an accurate picture of what's going on at your Airbnb. Is one guest playing really loud music or is there a full on party?

---

40   help.noiseaware.io/best-practices/rental-agreement-language

You need a strong Wi-Fi signal to ensure proper and timely data transmission. Believe it or not, many listings lack this feature. You may need to purchase a Wi-Fi booster (amzn.to/2igAV7d). There's a chance that your Wi-Fi signal is so low that you may not be able to use the product at all.

NoiseAware's sensors are not manufactured to be used outdoors. However, if you use them outdoors and they damage, NoiseAware will replace for free. To avoid that back and forth, place outlet covers on any sensors you choose to place outdoors. I confirmed with the NoiseAware team that an outdoor device is in the works.

Party Squasher can be somewhat unreliable as to knowing how many devices are in your home. This is especially true for apartment/condo owners where everyone is squished so close. The device could be picking up your neighbors. This is why I set my alarm for 3x my occupancy and lower the sensor setting to lowest. The highest setting covers up to 125 feet (38 meters).

Pricing

NoiseAware charges a one-time hardware and annual software cost. Each sensor costs $99 for the hardware with an annual fee of $99 for ongoing monitoring. A sensor covers a property's "activity zones", areas in your property where guest may congregate and cause noise issues.

All in with a sensor and their monitoring service, NoiseAware's noise monitoring solution is under $200 for the year.

Party Squasher charges $149 for the hardware with an optional $99 per year premium subscription. Having both breaks down to about $30 a month.

Customer Service

NoiseAware has that live chat box in the lower-right corner that I love! They even have automatic chat popups when you go to pages where you're likely to need assistance, like the support page. Otherwise, you can email Support@NoiseAware.io.

Party Squasher provides a contact form directly on the website with a phone number. Their support email is support@partysquasher.com.

Overall Recommendation

Overall, monitoring your Airbnb in a privacy-safe way has proven to be surprisingly valuable to me. I didn't even know this technology existed a year ago. Reading articles in the news on cities that point the finger at "party houses" and noise issues of short term rentals makes me realize that preventing the problem from ever happening is more important now than ever.

Rent Responsibly

While NoiseAware's mission is to prevent unnecessary noise pollution, they're also fiercely committed to saving the short-term rental industry and urging cities to implement fair regulation. The advocacy arm of their company, Rent Responsibly, serves to help cities understand how to implement fair regulation and keep the sharing economy alive. Rent Responsibly (www.rentresponsibly.org) is a campaign for all within the industry to educate, advocate, and celebrate the positive impacts of short-term rentals.

CHAPTER 29

Book Reviews

There are two biographical books on the market right now where the authors had access to Airbnb and the Co-founders. I read both and thought it would be fun (and hopefully you're interested!) to include them here. You can find full reviews on my website blog at www.OptimizeMyAirbnb.com/Blog.

The Upstarts *by Brad Stone*

OptimizeMyAirbnb.com Rating: 9/10

Amazon Rating (as of December 2017): 4.7 of 5 from 107 reviews

I devoured The Upstarts in 11 days. Ironically, mostly in the back of Lyft and Uber's on the way to one of the properties I manage on Airbnb in San Francisco.

This book dives deeper into fewer issues in the nine-year history of both companies rather than covering a vast amount of topics with little detail. Kind of reminds me of this book, a deep dive into specific Airbnb strategies rather than a general overview for beginners.

Even though Airbnb and Uber are in the title of the book, it must have been about 70% Uber.

Overall, I felt the book was really well researched and well together from a storyline point of view. The Uber/Airbnb stories crisscrossed nicely. Actually, I was surprised at the amount of overlap from the founders both attending the 2008 presidential inauguration (though, from very different perspectives) to friendships formed between Chesky and Kalanick in the early days that last through today.

The book didn't try to cover every topic over the past 8 years. Instead Brad Stone focused on fewer topics while adding more substance to them. As a prior Airbnb employee and an early adopter of both Lyft and Uber, I still learned much from reading this book. Not to mention it was entertaining and more so based on storytelling rather than analyzing past events.

I was pleased to learn that my memory of history is accurate (well, kind of). The Uber as we know it today has Lyft to thank. In 2012 when Lyft put those pink mustaches on their cars in San Francisco and popularized ride-sharing as we know it today, Uber was still a black car service for rich people. Uber copied Lyft about six months later and started allowing anyone to drive while offering lower cost alternatives to passengers. In reality, SideCar beat Lyft by about 2 months, but they no longer exist.

The book went into an interesting history of Uber's Chinese competitor, Didi Kuaidi (which means 'honk-honk speedy' in English). It put some color to the news headlines, 'Uber loses in China, sells to Didi.'

A couple interesting facts:

1. Lyft was originally named Zimrides (short for Zimbabwe rides). Designer Harrison Bowden came up with 'Lyft'.
2. On New Years Eve 2015, 550K guests slept in Airbnbs; on NYE 2016, it was 1.3M; by the middle of 2016, 1.3M guests per night was the average.

The Airbnb Story *by Leigh Gallagher*

OptimizeMyAirbnb.com Rating: 7 out of 10

Amazon Rating (as of December 2017): 4.3 of 5 from 45 reviews

Leigh Gallagher's book is a behind-the-scenes story of Airbnb. It looks at the development of the online accommodation business that was created by Brian Chesky, Joe Gebbia, and Nathan Blecharczyk that has now grown into one of the world's most recognized and talked about brands.

Overall, The Airbnb Story was entertaining and I read the book from cover to cover. It is a book based on facts, there is little storytelling of the founders and their story. I felt it lacked depth. It covered many topics over the eight-year history of the company but did not provide a behind the scenes perspective, as I assumed it would, especially as the book was okayed by the three founders, giving Gallagher direct access to all of them and the company.

A couple interesting facts:

1. Airbnb is expected to earn $8.5B by 2020 (p. 199); When I left in 2015, revenue was well below $1B.
2. More than 70% of Airbnb stays are reviewed (p. 72).
3. Globally, more than 300,000 boutique hotels and bed-and-breakfasts are listed on Airbnb (p. 115).
4. As of late 2016, 1.4M guests and 45K listings are welcomed to the platform weekly (p. 199).

PART V

Bonus Content

CHAPTER 30

How to Put Your Airbnb on Autopilot

Key Points

▶ Initial setup of various software (pricing, electronic guidebooks, etc.) and hardware (keyless locks, etc.) is required.

▶ You'll have to hire a few local people including a cleaning team, emergency contacts, and repairmen.

▶ A quality cleaning team is crucial. They will also restock consumables.

▶ If you want to be 100% hands-off, you will need to hire a property manager. The below process will require up to an hour a week of your time.

I run a full-service Airbnb property management company (belopm. com)from anywhere in the world. Sometimes I have not seen the property in person before I start managing. My properties span from the east to the west coast of the United States of America and my process allows me to manage properties anywhere around the world.

This chapter will outline my process for minimizing work yet keeping both the guest and the host happy. It'll take a bit of setup, but most of the tools will need to be only slightly greased going forward. It depends on the property, but an hour per week is usually sufficient for a few properties.

The goal with this strategy is to anticipate and remedy guest complaints in advance and eliminate as much manual work as possible while still offering the guest a personalized experience.

PRO TIP: Silence bothers no one, but noise can drive people insane. To be as hands-off as possible, you must anticipate these intangibles and address early.

The first five sections will cover the online aspects of management and need to be completed before you host your first guest. The last four sections cover the offline aspects and are more management based.

With this self-management process in place, you will still have to:

- Answer one-off guest questions via message (For a cost, you can use www.VRFrontDesk.com or www.Guesty.com to eliminate this aspect.)
- Monitor pricing for rate and calendar optimization
- Update the software tools (rarely)
- Coordinate with the maintenance team
- Coordinate with Airbnb (in the case of a Host Guarantee claim)
- Maintain an optimized listing

Maintain an Optimized Listing

After reading this book, you will have the knowledge and skills to do this on your own. If specific questions arise, you can email me at Danny@OptimizeMyAirbnb.com. Maintaining an optimized listing will increase your conversion rate and decrease the number of questions you get right from the start. Remember to re-optimize at least semi-annually.

Setup Smartbnb

Smartbnb will automate up to 90% of your guest messages. Refer to Chapter 18: Optimizing and Automating Your Messages on how to do this. Also, you will need to create messages to automatically send to your cleaner and check in for any new, altered, or cancelled reservations. After initial setup, this tool will require infrequent maintenance.

Additionally, Smartbnb will automatically leave a positive guest review based on one of many templates you provide. Refer to Chapter 24: Smartbnb, Message Automation for a review and how to guide.

Setup Hostfully

This is crucial. Just as crucial as any other step. In the 100+ Airbnbs I've stayed in, no hosts have sent me an electronic guidebook and instead answered numerous of my questions. **Having an electronic guidebook will save you time and make you appear more professional.** After initial setup, this tool will require infrequent maintenance in the future. You will have this automatically sent to your guest via Smartbnb four days before check-in. Refer to Chapter 27: Hostfully, Electronic Guidebooks to learn more about Hostfully.

Setup NoiseAware

You must keep your neighbors happy (which in turn keeps your neighbors happy). This neat piece of hardware and software accurately tells you when the noise level in your home has increased to a point where it might start disturbing neighbors. By intercepting this issue early, you will save yourself time and money in the long run. After initial setup, your time will only be required to send a message or make a phone call to the guest on rare occasions when you receive an alert. Refer to Chapter 28: NoiseAware and Party Squasher, Noise Monitoring to learn more.

Setup PriceLabs

If your goal is to maximize occupancy and nightly rates, you need a smart pricing tool. There are many quality providers out there, but I prefer PriceLabs. They automatically update your calendar, plus allow for many customizations like allowing a guest book an orphan night or increasing your nightly minimum for reservations far into the future. After initial setup, I recommend monitoring on a weekly basis which takes about one minute.

Install an Electronic Lock

There might be more electronic lock options than Airbnb listings. I use this electronic lock: amzn.to/2hZV1SV. It is simple, easy to install, and gives zero headaches. If you want a more technologically advanced option, go to RemoteLock, they're official partners with Airbnb and offer some really neat solutions. Just know it'll require a bit of extra time up front to learn the software and install. In either case, you will communicate the access code to the guest with an automated message. Once set up, this requires virtually zero work. I recommend having a backup lockbox nearby with an extra set of keys. I use this lockbox: amzn.to/2yXB42F.

Hire a Cleaner

But, not just any cleaner. **This will be the hardest part of the entire setup process** and will directly result in your success or failure. You need a quality, responsible, timely cleaner. Do not provide linens. Your cleaner must maintain control over the entire process. Otherwise, you have to get involved with the laundromat when linens go missing or stained. Laundromats are stuck in the 80s with either zero accountability or a pen and paper method. Do not hire a budget cleaner. Their job is extremely tough, so you should pay them as such. Plus, you're going to require them to purchase and restock consumables. A budget cleaner will lead to subpar reviews, guest complaints, and a drain on your time in the following ways:

- Low quality cleaning job
- Not showing up on time or finishing late
- Using stained or mismatched linens
- Low attention to detail with things like folded towels and presentation
- Forgetting to do essential tasks specific to vacation rentals like restocking supplies, checking for damage, and opening windows so your guest can enter to natural light.

Get an Emergency Contact

This person will need to be available in times of emergency including mornings, nights, and weekends. Emergency situations are extremely rare with a bit of planning. Ideally, this will be the cleaner or someone who is already familiar with the property. You will communicate the emergency contact to the guest, but inform them to only reach out for true emergencies. All else should go through the host/co-host.

> **PRO TIP:** Refer to Airbnb.com/co-hosting for help from existing Airbnb hosts.

Hire a Repairs and Maintenance Team

Things will go wrong with your listing and eventually break. You don't have to secure a team in advance, but it's a good idea. If you're hosting a business traveler who isn't getting hot water in the morning, you want to be able to dispatch your contact right away. You may have to work out a deal with them where you pay extra for off hours, weekends, and urgent issues. **Hire local**, always. These guys are running a small business and they're very easy to work with. You could always get a handyman who can do almost anything, but there will come a time when you need a specialist. Here is a list of problems and who to call:

- Wi-Fi or cable is not working – Emergency contact or handyman (after you troubleshoot. Many times I solved the issue by having the guest plug it in)
- Heating or A/C – HVAC repairmen
- No hot water – plumber
- Clogged drains – plumber
- No light – electrician
- Lock issues – locksmith

Final Note

To be honest, the overall process goes a little deeper than this, but the above covers 90%+ without bogging you down in minute details. Some things can only be learned on the job. However, I'll provide one example here. It has to do with cancellation policies. I recommend a flexible cancellation policy as I believe Airbnb favors these listings. But, even if they did not, I would still have a flexible cancellation policy. I want flexibility as a guest and I want to give my guests flexibility. If I had a strict cancellation policy and the guest needed to cancel, they're likely going to reach out with a legitimate reason as to why they need to cancel and ask for a refund. At the least, you waste time exchanging a few extra emails and feel bad for not refunding them. At the most, you end up wasting time exchanging emails and refunding them in which case you should've just had a flexible cancellation policy to begin with.

To conclude, if you dread even the tiniest amount of customer service or guest interaction then above is not for you. But, I truly enjoy engaging with guests. It's fun to be an Airbnb host.

CHAPTER 31

17 Ways to Improve Your Hosting

1 Holiday decorations

This has a twofold benefit. If the guest is familiar with the holiday, the decorations make them feel at home. If the guest isn't familiar, the decorations make them feel like a local.

2. Banana pancakes

Add verbiage to the end of your listing asking the guest to write a code phrase with their inquiry. This ensures they read everything. My code word is 'banana pancakes'. When you receive a message without the code phrase, inform the guest that you find reservations go smoothest when you know the guest has read the entire listing.

3. Change 'away' to 'to'

I constantly see sentences like this: 25 minutes *away from* the airport. Instead say, 25min *to* airport. Not only is it easier to read, but it shifts the frame from how far your Airbnb is from the attraction to how close the attraction is to you. Said differently, the word choice subconsciously places the FPG in your Airbnb rather than in the airport.

4. Share an authentic meal with your guest

On my first night in Casablanca, the host ordered authentic Moroccan food and wine for us to share. This was awesome because I felt like a local, eating local food with a local. He even invited his local friend over to join!

5. Play music upon check-in

In addition to opening the windows for natural light and adding a scent, play some music for the guest. This puts you a step ahead of your competition. The cleaner can put it on when they leave. If you send a guest questionnaire, you can include 'what's your favorite music?'

6. Folded towels on bed

Along with the triangle crease in the toilet paper, fold the towels in an exciting shape rather than a square. I've seen some cleaners create cranes, but I think anything non-standard will do the trick, like rolls:

7. Create a Walk/Bike/Bus Map

If you live in a walkable, bikeable, or transit friendly city then create a simple map showing the guest how far they can get in 5, 10, and 20 minutes. Type your address into Google, screen print the image, highlight tourist attractions, indicate where your property is, and draw circles around your property while indicated that they represent 5, 10, and 20 minutes of travel time.

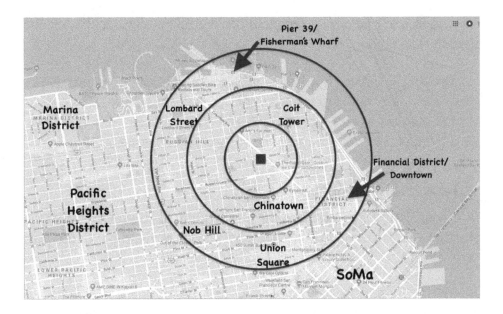

8. Add a floor plan to your photos

I use Floor Planner (floorplanner.com). This is especially important if you have multiple rooms with outdoor space or more than one story.

9. Car Rentals

EasyCar.com is a worldwide car rental search engine. It works everywhere. Literally. Add a link into the 'Directions' sub-section within the 'Guest Resources' section.

10. Live Check-In

Ideally, you are setup for a self check-in with the option of a live check-in. Most guests will choose the self check-in option. Just remember, if you do a live check-in, don't take more than 10 minutes. Anything you say should be accessible in the electronic guidebook for the guest to reference later. You should tell this to the guest so they don't stress about remembering everything. After a day of travel, the guest's mind is not suitable to absorb 30 minutes of instruction. Use the time to highlight very important house rules, how to operate tricky amenities, and one or two personalized recommendations that can be used at that time.

> **PRO TIP:** If a guest uses Instant Book and doesn't send another message, they're going to prefer a self check-in. On the other hand, if a guest asks for recommendations, etc. they might prefer a live check-in. Wow them by offering before they ask.

11. Tourist Attraction Guides

If your listing is frequented by guests going to the same tourist attraction (i.e. Disneyland), include physical Disneyland park guides in your Airbnb.

12. Live Check-Outs

Saying good-bye to your guest upon check-out is underrated. It makes for a positive last impression and you can answer any travel/flight details in person. People are usually stressed out on travel days so having a local who is familiar with the airport answer questions is invaluable. Additionally, you can ask for feedback in person and specify how you will address any issues that came up during their reservation. Consider offering a departing gift.

In the rare case of a negative stay, you should prioritize meeting the guest upon check-out as it's a lot easier to hold negative feelings towards a virtual screen than in person. Often those negative feelings dissipate once the guest meets you in person and see's how nice you are. At that point, the guest will be reviewing you as a person just as much as the property. It's a lot harder for someone to negatively review a person than a property.

13. Early Check-in Requests

Very rarely do I allow a guest to check-in early. If the unit is not cleaned, they cannot see it. The main reason is it creates a bad first impression entering into a dirty home, sometimes excessively dirty. A secondary reason is that the guest may notice something while dropping off their luggage and specifically check it upon their return (i.e. why didn't that pillow move? The place must be dirty!).

> **PRO TIP:** If you cannot or do not want to accommodate a late check-out, inform the requesting guest that you already con-firmed an early check-in for the same day and allowing a late check-out will be too hard on your cleaners.

14. Guest Communication

If something has changed about your Airbnb either good (i.e. Uber is now legal) or bad (i.e. construction started next door), inform the guest prior to arrival.

15. Finicky Locks

If for some reasons you do not have an electronic lock and there is a special wiggle to get the lock to open, you must either demonstrate in person or via video. If in person, have the guest try locking it once.

16. Spend a weekend in your listing

Do this twice per year. And, be sure to cook a meal in the kitchen and use all available amenities. You will always find repairs that need to be made or additions to further increase the guest experience. Often, you will find a non working light bulb. As the cleaners are there during the day, no one notices when lights go out. Additionally, a cleaner may forget to tell you about a slow draining faucet or shower drain.

17. PleaseLeaveA5*Review

Change your wi-fi password to something like this. Not only does the length, special character, and capital letters make it secure, but also it's easy to remember. Your guest will thank you when they input it on multiple devices and share it with the other guests to put into their multiple devices. At the very least, it should give your guest an early chuckle upon check-in and remind them of your expectations.

CHAPTER 32

How to Identify Problem Guests Before They Book

Key Points

- ▶ Reviews are the most important factor, by far. Other than reviews, an incomplete guest profile positively correlates with a poor guest experience.
- ▶ Up to 40% of reservations are from new guests. If you receive an inquiry from an incomplete guest profile, ask them to complete more of it.
- ▶ The content of the message thread is important to consider if you're not sure about the guest.
- ▶ A live check-in allows you to detect any red flags based on the guest behavior.

I**t all comes down to how complete the Airbnb guests profile is.** Did the guest do the bare minimum to setup a profile? Did he or she spend time poking around the website and filling in the optional profile fields? Or, does the profile land somewhere in between? As an Airbnb property manager, I've encountered thousands of profiles and noticed a common theme: an incomplete profile correlates to a bad guest experience.

To clarify, a "bad guest experience" does not mean that you did not get along with the guest personally. It also does not mean that a guest made some late night noise that disturbed a neighbor. A bad guest experience means a more serious situation that causes damage to the property or the host. This could range from a guest who invites uncon-firmed friends for a party or leaves the house extra dirty, to a thief who makes a reservation for the sole purpose of robbing the host. It's important for me to note that **these instances are extremely uncommon, a fraction of a percent.** How-ever, bad guest experiences do happen so as a host, you want to turn over every stone to avoid ending up in that fraction of a percent.

> A bad guest experience is a serious situation that causes damage to the property or the host.

In the first part of this chapter, I'll show you a complete profile and explain each of the thirteen sections. Then, I'll show you a profile that meets the bare minimum stan-dard. Next, I'll point out which parts of the profile are most important and why (spoiler alert: a verified ID is not #1). Lastly, I'll give you some tips on how to identify potential prob-lem Airbnb guests based on profile alone and strategies to encourage guests to complete their profiles.

Like I mentioned above, **there are thirteen parts to complete a profile.** Below is a 100% completed profile (yes, it's me! I'm now a Superhost with almost 200 reviews, but to keep it realistic, a guest inquiring will not be a Superhost.).

If I requested to stay at my listing, I would happily and easily accept because I went above and beyond to complete the profile.

Let's examine each section of my profile:

1. The profile photo is a close-up of me, and it's not blurry.
2. I listed my real first name.
3. I identified my current city or where I'm from.

4. I created my profile many years ago (note: this is automatically populated in any profile; however, it's an important piece of information).
5. I verified myself multiple ways.
6. My description is more than 100 words. (Refer to Chapter 20: Improve Your Airbnb Profile For More Guests)
7. Hosts have reviewed me (and, in my case, guests also reviewed me).
8. References vouched for me.
9. I verified my offline ID.
10. I provided additional information about myself.
11. I created at least one Airbnb Wish List.
12. I'm a host.
13. I created at least one Airbnb guidebook.

We'll get into each section and which are most important soon. Now, let's look at an incomplete profile—one that can't be any less complete.

How many sections are complete on this profile? Trick question. The answer is zero. The profile photo (1) is not ideal because we cannot see the person. The name (2) does not count because, well, "D" is not a full name. The guest did not identify a location (3) because Airbnb defaults to "US" based on IP address. The verifications (5) are incomplete because you must verify an email address and phone number to register with Airbnb. If a person with this profile sent me a request, I would deny it.

Towards the end of this chapter, I'll touch on a strategy that shows how, as a host, you can encourage a guest to complete his or her profile. This will put you at ease when managing requests from Airbnb guests with brand new profiles.

Before I discuss how you can encourage Airbnb guests to complete profiles, I'd like to rank each profile section in order of importance. The number inside the parenthesis refers to the section of the profile as identified above.

1. **Reviews (7)** - If other hosts reviewed the guest, this gives you a clear indication of who they are as a guest. If they have reviews from other guests, it means they're also a host— **this is the holy grail of Airbnb guests** because they know what it's like to be a host. Obviously, you should ensure the reviews are positive or that they responded appropriately if the reviews are negative.

2. **Hosting (12)** - If the guest is also a host, she knows what it's like to be in your shoes. You should look at her reviews to check for positive feedback.

3. **Date (4)** - Though the profile automatically populates this field, it's extremely important when it comes to Airbnb guests who may be thieves trying to rob you—thieves don't plan months or years in advance. Let's say you lost your wallet, a thief recovered it, created an Airbnb profile, and even verified the ID. If the thief were smart, he would put up a nice photo and fill in a name, location, and description. However, with a recently created account, the profile may still lack reviews. Profiles without reviews raise red flags for me. However, Airbnb gets so many new guests every day that profiles without reviews are

common. In scenarios like this, review the remainder of the profile for completeness.

4. **Verifications (5)** - The bare minimum verifications are phone number and email address. When you start seeing Facebook, LinkedIn, American Express, Offline ID, and so forth, the guest went above minimum standards.

5. **Verified ID (9)** - Verified ID is important but because a thief can verify any ID, it shouldn't be as important to a host as other elements of a guest profile. In conjunction with a completed profile that's a few months old, a verified ID is a powerful piece of information.

6. **Description (6)** - You can tell a lot about someone through his or her writing. A profile without any writing raises a sizeable red flag, whereas a profile with a description of less than 50 words raises a small red flag. Anything around 100 words is great. For reference, my profile is 217 words and probably on the longer end. Refer to Chapter 21: How To Complete 100% of Your Host Profile to learn how to craft a perfect Airbnb profile description.

7. **Photo (1)** - A photo is not as important because anyone can add a photo, and Airbnb does not verify identity through photos. However, is the photo blurry? Is it of a group? Is it of the sunset? Is it a drawing? If it's anything but a clear and up-close photo of a guest, this would raise a red flag.

8. **About Me (10)** - Has the guest taken time to fill in his work, school, and language? If not, it might raise a red flag, depending on what else he completed on the profile. If he completes the About Me section, he went above and beyond the minimums. It's great if this section is complete but if it's not, I would scrutinize the rest of the profile.

9. **References (8)** - Here's information that gives you a glimpse into the guest's personality and means the guest went above and beyond the bare minimums.

10. **Location (3)** - Does the profile display "US" or any other country only? This means the guest left the location field blank, and

Airbnb populated the field based on IP address. Or did the guest enter a location? If you live in a volatile Airbnb market like New York, Barcelona, San Francisco then I recommend you change your city to someplace nearby that's pro-Airbnb. This is especially true if you have multiple listings. You never know who's scraping the website for data on hosts in certain cities.

11. **Name (2)** - Although this is not as important, a red flag should raise if the guest's name is something like 'xyz' or 'D'. The guest can type any name, and it's not necessary to match the profile name with the verified identity. Overall, this would give you another bit of information about the guest if the name is anything but, well, a name.

12. **Wish List (11)** - This is totally optional, but a wish list means the guest has taken some time to poke around the system and observe the website and its features.

13. **Guidebook (13)** - This is only applicable if the guest is also a host. This section means the host created a guidebook for their Airbnb guests. It's not highly used or highlighted on Airbnb, so a lot of good hosts do not use this feature. If the guidebook is there, it would give me increased confidence in the guest, but not having one is not a red flag.

At what point is a profile complete enough to not raise any red flags? It really comes down to two questions:

1. Has the guest been reviewed by other hosts?
2. Has the guest been reviewed by other guests?

Reviews are the most important section of any profile, hands down. If the guest has more than three reviews as either a guest or a host in the past 12 months, it's a safe bet.

NOTE: Your book review is the most important part of my book profile. Please consider leaving one for me to read. Or, share your thoughts directly to me at Danny@OptimizeMyAirbnb.com.

The decision gets subjective when the guest does not have any reviews. In these cases, I defer to the 11 remaining sections of the profile

(3-13). I consider nine of these sections important (1, 2, 3, 4, 5, 6, 8, 9, and 10). Eight are immediately editable by a guest who's just created their profile (4 is not editable). Barring any egregious items on the profile, I would accept any guest who has at least seven sections complete.

For clarification, egregious items are, in no particular order:

The description is hateful or distasteful.

References speak negatively of the guest.

The name appears to be hiding the guest's identity.

. . .

If all else fails and you're still unsure, consider accepting and doing a live check-in.

. . .

If five or six sections are filled in, I would defer to my judgment and to the complete versus incomplete parts of the profile. If four or less sections are filled in, **I ask the guest to complete the profile.** I write something like this:

"I'd like to know more about you before accepting the reservation; do you mind completing your profile, including verifying your ID? This can be found at www.Airbnb.com/Verify."

Typically, the guest will respond that she was in a hurry and will finish the profile when she gets home, or something along those lines. If the guest responds negatively, this should be considered a red flag.

One aspect of the reservation process that I left out is the message thread. **The message thread is equally important as the profile** for the same reason why the description is important—you can tell a lot about someone by how he writes. If the messages are extremely short or sound suspicious, ask more questions to get a feel for who he is and the purpose of the trip.

If all else fails and you're still unsure, consider accepting and doing a live check-in. Don't inform the guest in advance of your live check-in. Meeting the guest face-to-face will allow you to detect any red flag indications from their behavior or attitude.

These are strategies I've developed over the past three years as a host and Airbnb property manager.

CHAPTER 33

How to Write a Proper Review

Key Points

▶ Retaliation is not possible due to Airbnb review system being double-blinded

▶ You have 48 hours to edit your review unless the other party left their review in that time or the 14 day review window expired.

▶ If you plan to leave a negative review, ensure you follow all guidelines so Airbnb does not remove it

Airbnb hosts and guests stress about writing an Airbnb review when the reservation doesn't go perfectly. And, eventually, a reservation won't go perfectly. I'm going to provide you a review template to use for all of your future Airbnb experiences, both positive and negative as either a host or guest.

> PRO TIP: Read your reviews. So many hosts ignore them especially as they get more listings. Guests are brutally honest, especially in the private feedback area. Take any negative as an opportunity to improve.

The Airbnb review system[41] is double blinded. The host/guest do not see the review until either both have written a review or one has written a review and 14 days have passed (the time Airbnb allows you to

---

41 www.airbnb.com/help/article/13/how-do-reviews-work

write the review). **You have 48 hours to edit your review** unless the other party has already reviewed you or the 14-day time limit passed. Keep in mind if you travel in a group, you will get the review published on your profile even if you didn't make the reservation.

How to write an Airbnb review for your host (as an Airbnb guest)

This template works for both positive and negative reviews. First, put your overall star score because Airbnb does not show this for some reason. Then, the length of your stay. Then list the pros. Then list the cons. Done. It is as simple as that. This format can also be used by an Airbnb host to review their guest.

Here's what it looks like in the wild:

Daniel Rusteen
November 2017

OVERALL: ★★★★★ STAY: 1 night PROS: Smooth check-in, luxurious backyard with pool, convenient for walking to shops/restaurants/beach, staff are super helpful for anything, friendly host CONS: Nothing significant

How to write a negative Airbnb review for your guest (as an Airbnb host)

I encourage you to be truthful (and concise). A lot of hosts avoid putting anything overly negative in a guest review. I'm not sure why. If you fall in this category of Airbnb host then **a short review is the same as a negative review.** If I see a guest with a review like 'good guest' or 'checked out timely' then I assume this is really a negative review from a host who does not want to leave an honest review.

Here's what that looks like:

How to write a positive Airbnb review for your guest (as an Airbnb host)

This should be pretty obvious, right? There's a lot of systems out there (i.e. Smartbnb) that will automatically write your guest a generic positive review. To be honest, this is satisfactory. Airbnb has stated that leaving reviews does not affect your search rank. Still, I recommend leaving reviews, but length and variation make no difference. As a host, you want to know the guest treated other hosts' space with respect, obeyed the house rules, and left the place undamaged.

Include your Airbnb's title in the review for added branding and to get your name out there more (i.e. Daniel was a fantastic guest at Super Duper Airbnb House)

Negative Review Advice

Airbnb will remove reviews, especially negative reviews if all terms of service are not followed. Airbnb knows that a guest with a negative review is unlikely to have future success making reservations. Airbnb cannot profit from a guest who cannot make a reservation. If you're an experienced Airbnb host, you may have encountered this. Your review got removed due to a technicality in the terms of service or review guidelines. It can be very frustrating as you want other hosts to know about your negative experience. Its best to avoid talking about reviews at all with your guest when the experience turns negative.

CHAPTER 34

Slow Season Strategies

Key Points

- ▶ A proper slow season strategy requires year-round attention.
- ▶ A good strategy includes a combination of techniques applied to pricing, title, nightly minimums, and calendar availability.
- ▶ You probably need to lower your price more. It should fluctuate 40%+ over the year. Any decrease in price is going to have the largest and most immediate effect on your search rank.

D o you have a customized annual Airbnb slow season pricing strategy?

I found the vast majority of hosts do not have an active yearly pricing strategy in place other than lowering the rate when it is already too late. Some hosts apply a haphazard strategy throughout the year. Then, complain of no reservations during slow season.

If you follow the below Airbnb slow season strategies, you will be setting yourself above your competition and allow yourself to cruise straight through your slow season.

There are numerous slow season strategies you can implement throughout the year. Some of these strategies have you planning six months in advance. It depends on your situation, but you should follow at least half of the below strategies. The Airbnb listings I manage, follow all of them.

Add the Word "Discount" to Your Airbnb Title

☆☆**New Listing Discount 15%**☆☆
Balcony ☆ Parking ☆

Veronika

Tallinn, Harju maakond, Estonia ★ ★ ★ ★ ★ 3 reviews

Refer to Chapter 4: Mastering the Title for a more in-depth discussion about your title. Specifically, for slow season, you can add verbiage into your title like 'Extra 10% Discount'. I see this so rarely that it will get FPGs to click on your listing, at the very least.

The idea being that a guest has already narrowed down your listing to their ideal budget and then seeing you offer an extra 10% discount, they would be crazy not to have a look.

Be sure to specify the details of this discount in your listing description. If it works well, you might consider increasing your pricing to offset the discount a bit or using it as one of your year-round season strategies. The downside to using this strategy is that it will require you to manually send the FPG a special offer.

> **PRO TIP:** Offer discounts to certain groups: Firefighters, military, teachers, etc. As this will only apply to a minority of guests, add the verbiage to the 'Other things to note' text section.

Offer a 'Friends + Family' Airbnb Discount

One automated way to increase bookings is to use a service like Smartbnb to send out an automatic message to the guest a week after check-out letting them know that you offer an extra X% discount to the guest and their friends and family (as long as they mention the guest by name) during slow season.

You can get creative and offer the discount for only midweek stays, for stays of four days or longer, for stays on any day in particular months, etc.

Increase Percentage Discounts

There's a reason the first three sections have to do with pricing. You probably aren't lowering your pricing enough during slow season. And, Airbnb favors with a rank increase every dollar you lower your pricing. Take advantage of it.

To attract long-term guests, increase monthly and weekly booking discounts. In general, a week gets a 10-20% discount and a month gets a 20-40% discount. If you have time to be more detailed, go into Airbnb.com and research your competition. Filter the search for your area, price range, and number of beds to see how much they are offering for a discount and beat them out by 5%+.

Adjust Your Airbnb Pricing Hack

If you already follow the strategy outlined in Chapter 8: Pricing Hack For More Views then tweaking it will be easy. Re-measure your average pricing (it will be lower in the slow season than high season) and set your 'Base price' in Airbnb to about 10% lower.

Adjust Calendar Availability

In general, I recommend Airbnb hosts to keep their calendar open six months into the future. This is because you can charge a premium to guests booking 3+ months out, but a guest booking 6+ months in advance probably knows something that you do not (i.e. upcoming conference, concert, etc.).

With this strategy, I suggest you open your calendar availability to 12 months at the start of busy season. Three months later, adjust your availability to nine months. Three months later, adjust to six months. This strategy, though not perfect due to Airbnb limitations, essentially allows guests to book through next years slow season where price maximization is much less a concern than occupancy rate.

The concept behind this strategy is to secure some bonus reservations from the guests who are planning ahead 6+ months in advance of Airbnb slow season. If you have 5 days booked on a few of your slow season months, this relieves a lot of pressure.

Remove Extra Person Charges

Using an extra person charge is an aggressive pricing strategy best kept for high season. Most hosts incur limited additional cost with an added guest, yet most charge for an extra person simply because it is an option. Remove the extra person charge during your slower months.

However, I recommend adding a significant extra person charge for any guest over your maximum. For example, if your maximum occupancy is set for 4 guests, add a $100 charge for guests after 4. This accomplishes two things. First, it allows Airbnb to allow you to charge the guest if they bring more than allowed. Otherwise, Airbnb will agree that there were more guests, but will not send you any extra money because you do not indicate any charge for additional guests. Second, it disincentives the guest from bringing extra people in the first place.

On the flip side, if you are hosting an entire home and you are not on the premise, but charging for extra guests before your maximum (in the example above, let's say you charge $10 for the 3rd and 4th guest), some guests will simply put two guests to avoid the charge for the 3rd and 4th. Instead, I recommend you price your space for maximum occupancy which is what most guests are looking for anyways.

In high season when demand overcomes supply, you are able to be more aggressive with your pricing by adding in an extra person charge. Keep in mind that if you rent your listing to four people at $100 per night, each person is paying $25 per night. If you add in an extra person charge for a 5th guest (add a floor mattress or pull-out sofa), this fee should be a maximum of $25 on the high end. I recommend you charge around 50% of the cost per person without an added guest. In this case, 50% of $25 is $12.50 which is closer to the incremental costs you will incur with that additional guest.

> • • •
>
> I recommend adding a significant extra person charge for any guest over your maximum.
>
> • • •

Lower Minimum Nights

I recommend a year-round one-night minimum. However, if you have a 2+ night minimum, the Airbnb slow season would be a great time to test out a single night minimum, even if it is just for weekdays. Most cleaners would gladly accept the additional work.

Although I recommend a single-night minimum, the cleaning fee can be used to deter single night reservations. The percentage of cleaning cost to overall booking cost increases with fewer nights. To test out a one-night minimum, increase your cleaning fee by 20%. A two- or three-night reservation would barely notice the increase, but a one-night reservation would.

Lower Your Night Rate

Obviously, right? But, lower it more than you think. Hotels lower prices up to 40% during slow season and they are professionals with numerous marketing channels and teams devoted to getting the pricing right. You need to understand your fixed costs (expenses paid regardless of a guest occupying your space like rent or mortgage) and variable costs (expenses paid only when a guest is in your space like electricity) to know what your true minimum price should be.

Your minimum represents the amount you would accept for a reservation that allows you to profit instead of keeping the place vacant. It should equal your fixed costs plus variable costs for the reservation plus a reasonable profit margin that takes into account your time. A minimum is not what you would like to get. A lot of hosts make this mistake and price their minimum way too high during the Airbnb slow season.

Airbnb Slow Season Strategies Conclusion

You need an active annual pricing strategy to account for the low and high seasons. Due to demand, anyone can get by in high season, but it is the Airbnb slow season that separates the professionals from the amateurs. Here is what you should think about in order of importance:

1. Lower your nightly rate up to 40%+.
2. Adjust your calendar availability to encourage early slow season bookings.

3. Adjust your base price within Airbnb related to the Airbnb pricing hack.
4. Increase your percentage discounts based on competition.
5. Remove extra person charge.
6. Lower minimum nights to one.
7. Add the word 'Discount' into the front of your title.
8. Offer a 'Friends + Family' Airbnb discount.

For kicks, here's what Airbnb has to say about how to navigate the slow season... blog.atairbnb.com/travel-seasonality/

CHAPTER 35

Creating Additional Revenue Streams

There are so many ways to create additional streams of revenue, yet few hosts leverage this. If you're a host, then you're running a business. Think like a business(wo)man. I have ordered this list in order of the time commitment involved to implement.

Increase Average Reservation Length

Increase weekend pricing while lowering Thursday/Sunday night pricing is a strategy that results in slightly longer stays on average due to some guests adding on an extra 'cheap' weekday. You'll find that all good pricing tools do this automatically for you.

> **PRO TIP:** If you have an un-booked day on either side of a reservation you can use Smartbnb to automatically send a message to the guest offering a small discount to extend.

Add Referral Codes into your Listing

Uber, Lyft, food delivery, etc. Add some of them into your listing. Usually the guest will get something free, as well as, the host. A win-win.

Apply for the Airbnb Super Referral Program

Available to hosts across the globe, you can refer Airbnb hosts and earn $300 as opposed to the standard $100 in the past. You have to apply and be accepted into this program.[42]

Provide Souvenirs

Lots of travelers on vacation want to bring back some souvenirs for their friends and family. But, what if they forget or don't have time or just prefer not to haggle at the markets? Have some *unique* souvenirs the guest can purchase from you. Provide some cheap, free souvenirs, but also offer betters ones for purchase. You can mention this in your electronic guidebook and host profile.

Send a Guest Questionnaire

This has the two-fold benefit of increasing their experience (celebrating anything, favorite, type of wine for welcome gift, etc.) plus upselling them on additional services (airport pickup, fridge stocking, hire a chef, etc.).

Showcase your Art

If you're an artist, a great way to earn some extra income is to showcase your paintings. I would not add price tags to the artwork, but instead mention this in the electronic guidebook and wait for the interested guest to ask.

Offer an Airport Transfer

Either offer to pickup the guest yourself or secure a deal with a local airport transfer company. In either case, clarify the price up front.

Charge For Early Check-ins/Late Check-Outs

If a guest wants to check-in 30 minutes early, then you should not try to charge for this. But, if a guest wants to check-in 2+ hours early, I think it's reasonable to charge a bit extra. You can use GuestBook,

---

42   https://goo.gl/BkHDmu

a property management software, to do this automatically (useguest-book.com). Otherwise, you can use Airbnb to charge the guest extra.

Offer Additional Services

Brainstorm a bit and come up with a list of 4-5 additional services your guests may benefit from including a cooking class, a hired chef, laundry or dry cleaning service, pre-stocking the fridge, tickets to local activities, or restaurant reservations. Think of routine errands the guest must do upon arrival. Think, how can you save the guest some time?

Rent Your Car

There's many companies that allow you to rent your personal car. In the United States, there's Getaround (www.getaround.com/invite/3628316), Turo (turo.com/c/dannyr380), and a bunch more. You can find other companies offering the same thing across the globe.

Earn a Commissions on Local Activities

Find two or three *unique*, local experiences the guest wouldn't find had they researched online for 30 minutes prior to arriving. Work out a deal with the provider where you'll earn a small commission for every guest you send their way.

> PRO TIP: Avoid listing either too many or common nearby attractions in your listing. If they're common, the guest already knows about them. If too many, you're taking the guest attention away from sellable features of your listing. Your Airbnb listing is not a trip planner.

Collect Guest Personal Emails

This is more effective if you have many Airbnb listings, but you can collect personal email addresses of prior guests to target them with future promotions. Be sure to get their permission first. Services like Smartbnb and Guesty do this automatically.

CHAPTER 36

How Safe Is Airbnb?

Key Points

▶ Only a tiny fraction of reservations have serious issues that require immediate attention from Airbnb. If we compare to the hotel industry, Airbnb is much safer.

▶ Read Chapter 32: How to Identify Problem Guests Before They Book

▶ Check out this Chrome extension for Airbnb that allows a host to see how a guest reviewed prior hosts.

▶ It is likely Airbnb gives a boost to listings with more safety features as a risk mitigation strategy.

I t is no secret that Airbnb can save you money as a guest and line your pocket with cash as a host. But some people still have reservations about the whole thing. The big question? *Safety.*

Isn't it safer as a traveler to stay in a hotel rather than some random person's home, you might ask? And as a homeowner, how do I know guests are not going to completely trash my place or run off with everything but the doorknobs?

In other words: *just how safe is Airbnb?*

Can You Trust People?

Unfortunately not everyone in the world can be trusted. Once we accept and acknowledge this reality it becomes a question of filtering through the ones we can. See Chapter 32: How to Identify Problem Airbnb Guests Before They Book.

Airbnb is actually a great platform for filting because of the tools they create for this purpose:

Airbnb ID verification

Airbnb has a process to help confirm the identity of users. It connects a user with their Facebook profile, phone number, email address, government-issued ID, and even uses photo recognition software to check that their Airbnb profile photo and official ID (such as passport photo) are of the same person. While it is not foolproof, verification does help keep the community safer.

Hosts can select to only allow guests who are verified (as long as the host has verified themselves) to make reservations. Guests can also check hosts profiles for the green verified badge.

Airbnb review system

How else do you know you can trust someone? By reading their reviews.

See related Chapter 33: How To Write A Proper Airbnb Review.

Hosts and guests both get reviewed on Airbnb. If someone has a hundred glowing reviews it is with good reason. If they have negative reviews be sure to read them and try to judge whether they truly reflect the person's character or are just one-off outliers.

Hosts, in particular, rely on good reviews for their own business, so the system is very effective at keeping people accountable.

There is a Chrome extension for Airbnb[43] that shows you what the Airbnb guest said in their review of prior hosts.

Airbnb Trust & Safety team

As a company, Airbnb dedicates a lot of resources to trust and safety. A team of full-time staff are available 24/7 to respond to any issues experienced by either guests or hosts, before, during, or after the reservation. A quick search of 'trust and safety Airbnb' on LinkedIn brings up over 650 profiles. You see titles with 'proactive', 'reactive', and 'investigator'.

---

43   goo.gl/RDgkzY

Part of their job is also keeping the Airbnb community free of illegal activity (like money laundering, illicit substances, and prostitution) and high-risk guests[44].

What you can do: check for the "Verified" stamp and read the reviews before booking / accepting someone. Hosts can also vet guests by asking them questions to find out more about who they are and why they are visiting the area. Most guests are forthcoming with this information, but the few that are not should raise red flags.

What About Theft and Damages?

For hosts:

Let's say you have vetted your guests as best you can and yet something still goes wrong.

Many countries are now covered by Airbnb's own Host Protection Insurance[45], which protects against liability claims up to the value of $1 million. This is a huge commitment from Airbnb, but it does have caveats. Hosts can rest easier knowing Host Protection exists — but they should considering their own insurance depending on the circumstances. Refer to Chapter 37: Airbnb Host Insurance Information to learn more about Airbnb's insurance policies.

For guests:

A common concern is that personal belongings will not be as safe at an Airbnb as at a hotel, and that hosts may not be insured if something goes wrong. While it is true that hotels take security measures including in-room safes (Airbnb hosts should have these, too), a lot of people fail to realize hotels also tend to wash their hands of any liability. Here is an example of a hotel security policy[46] from a Sheraton hotel (bold parts added for emphasis):

"THE HOTEL IS **NOT RESPONSIBLE FOR LOSS, DAMAGE OR THEFT** OF CASH, JEWELRY OR OTHER VALUABLES

---

44   time.com/4890986/airbnb-alt-right-virginia-rally
45   goo.gl/mtXKwa
46   goo.gl/ScBLyC

LEFT UNATTENDED IN GUEST ROOMS. SAFE DEPOSIT BOXES ARE AVAILABLE FOR THE SAFEKEEPING OF THESE ITEMS. THE HOTEL'S LIABILITY REGARDING ITEMS IN THE SAFE DEPOSIT BOX IS **LIMITED TO THE EQUIVALENT OF THE RATE OF** A ONE **NIGHT** STAY."

Such hotel policies are not all that comforting. Either way, if you are traveling it is always best to have your own insurance as well.

What you can do: If you are a host, make sure you have vacation rental insurance coverage on your property and its contents. Keep valuable and irreplaceable items locked up in a secure area or take them off-site. If you are a guest, be covered by your own travel insurance as much as possible.

Protection From Fires and Gas Leaks

Airbnb is putting in a lot of effort into making safety features a standard for properties — especially smoke and CO detectors. While it is difficult for them to police these features or verify that they are installed, they do make sure it is in the host's interest to have them.

Firstly, potential guests can check the list of safety features in a home before booking and therefore avoid properties that do not have them. A second incentive for hosts is that CO and smoke detectors are mandatory features for getting "Business Travel Ready" status. It's plausible that Airbnb might favor listings in terms of search rank with more safety features installed as this lowers the chance of something going wrong

To show their commitment to the goal of making every property safer, Airbnb is actually giving away CO and smoke detectors to 36,000 eligible hosts, for free[47].

> **PRO TIP:** If you miss out on the above promotion, I recommend the highly rated Nest Smoke and Carbon Monoxide Alarm (amzn. to/2hE8DTN).

From a guest point of view this already makes Airbnb safer and more progressive than the hotel industry. In the U.S. alone more than 500

47   www.airbnb.com/home-safety

people die each year from carbon monoxide poisoning. According to the book *The Airbnb Story* by Leigh Gallagher, there were 68 incidents of carbon monoxide poisoning in U.S. hotels between 1989 and 2004, resulting in 27 deaths and 772 people accidentally poisoned. Disturbingly, only 13 U.S. states legally require the installation of CO detectors in hotels and motels[48].

Hotel fires are no less common: from 2009-2013, hotels averaged 3,520 fires per year resulting in 9 deaths.

What you can do: If you are a host, it is definitely in your interest to have smoke and carbon monoxide detectors installed. After all, you not only want more bookings to your property but you want to keep it and the people inside it safe from any potential harm. From a business perspective, **it is plausible Airbnb gives a boost to listings with more safety features as a risk mitigation strategy.**

As a guest, you can check the "Safety features" section of any Airbnb property before you book. Other safety features like fire extinguishers and first aid kits can also be listed in the property description.

So How Safe is Airbnb?

Airbnb horror stories do exist. Some guests are mistreated by hosts, some hosts have to endure nightmare guests. But let's be real here: humankind is far from perfect. You can be mugged in the safest city in the world or have an ugly experience at a world-class hotel, because nowhere and nothing in the world is 100% safe. Even places which seem safe may not be, especially if proper care is not taken.

It may seem harsh to put it like that, but that is the reality. It is beyond our control. What we *can* do is make decisions that mitigate the risks and give us the best safety and security possible.

Trust is the foundation of Airbnb and out of 100 million nights "less than a fraction of a percent have been problematic" said Airbnb co-founder Joe Gebbia in a highly-watched TED talk[49]. When trust works out right, says Gebbia, "it can be absolutely magical."

---

48   www.ncsl.org/research/environment-and-natural-resources/carbon-monox-ide-detectors-state-statutes.aspx

49   www.ted.com/talks/joe_gebbia_how_airbnb_designs_for_trust

With a little bit of faith, common sense and due vigilance, Airbnb is a safe, rewarding and positive experience for both guests and hosts.

CHAPTER 37

Airbnb Host Insurance Information

Key Points

- ▶ Host Protection Insurance is for claims of property damage or bodily injury and available to hosts in 15 countries. It is considered primary coverage.
- ▶ Host Guarantee is for property damage and is used for claims above the security deposit. A claim must be submitted before the next guest checks in.

I nsurance is confusing. This chapter is meant to give you an overview of the two insurances Airbnb provides you automatically while using their platform. I have read all of the relevant information from Airbnb regarding these two insurances and have either provided the text below or linked to it. You may, and probably should, get additional insurance and I have provided three companies who provide insurances specifically for Airbnb hosts. In the next chapter I have a Q+A with one the them.

Host Protection Insurance

This is primary liability (property damage or bodily injury) coverage of up to $1,000,000 per occurrence for both hosts and landlords in over 15 countries for claims that occur in the Airbnb listing or on the property during a reservation[50]. It may also cover claims related to building damage caused by the guest.

You can find detailed information of what is and is not covered on the Airbnb website[51]. You can email Airbnb[52] about the Host Protection Insurance (ensure you're logged in) or file a claim in the Resolution Center[53].

Common Questions (From Airbnb.com)

How does the Host Protection Insurance program work?

The Host Protection Insurance program provides coverage through a policy issued by certain underwriters at Lloyd's of London, and Zurich Insurance plc, two of the world's most reputable insurance providers.

When someone makes a claim against a host, a claim adjuster will administer and resolve the claim in accordance with policies agreed to with Airbnb.

Do I need to do anything to be covered under the Host Protection Insurance Program?

By agreeing to list a property, or continuing to list a property, on Airbnb you agree to be covered under the Host Protection Insurance program for occurrences during Airbnb stays, subject to the policy terms.

How does the Host Protection Insurance program work with my existing homeowner's or renter's insurance?

The Host Protection Insurance program will act as primary coverage for eligible losses.

---

50   www.airbnb.com/host-protection-insurance
51   www.airbnb.com/help/article/937/what-is-host-protection-insurance
52   www.airbnb.com/help/contact_us
53   https://www.airbnb.com/resolutions

How is this different than Airbnb's Host Guarantee?

Airbnb's Host Guarantee program is designed to protect hosts against damages to their own possessions or unit in the rare instance of property damage by their guests in listings.

Conversely, the Host Protection Insurance program is designed to protect hosts against third party claims of bodily injury or property damage.

How is this different than a security deposit?

Security deposits help cover accidents that occur during a reservation, like spilled wine on the rug, a broken window, or an unreturned key.

> **PRO TIP:** Regardless if you have a security deposit (SD) or not, you go through the same process within Airbnb to request money from the guest. If the guest denies, Airbnb gets involved. Still, I recommend you add a SD equal to the cost of one night stay as a deterrent against guests looking specifically for homes without a SD in place. Most guests are not aware that the SD actually makes no difference in terms of collection. Do not make your SD excessively high as this will scare away FPGs.

Host Guarantee

This is property damage coverage up to $1,000,000 available worldwide[54]. You make a claim through the resolution center. The Host Guarantee Program isn't insurance and doesn't replace your homeowners or renter's insurance.

The Host Guarantee Program doesn't cover cash and securities, collectibles, rare artwork, jewelry, pets or personal liability which is why I recommend you remove all of these things from your home prior to the first guest arrival.

You can find detailed terms on the Airbnb website[55].

---

54   https://www.airbnb.com/resolutions
55   www.airbnb.com/terms/host_guarantee

Common Questions (from Airbnb.com)

How does the Airbnb Host Guarantee process work?

When in an emergency situation, the host should first contact the police, emergency personnel, or the proper authorities. Then contact Customer Service[56].

When the situation is not an emergency, the host should contact the guest to notify them of the complaint and attempt to negotiate a resolution prior to filing an official claim.

If a resolution cannot be found between host and guest, the host should carefully review the Host Guarantee terms[57] and determine if they are eligible before submitting a request to Airbnb.

Hosts must submit their request either 14 days from the guest's check out, or before the next guest checks in, whichever is earlier.

For payment requests submitted on time, we'll send a confirmation email and follow up emails to discuss next steps–such as further documentation from the host or guest–within 24 hours.

Once we have received sufficient information from both the host and the guest, we'll review all documentation, evaluate the payment request, and contact the host upon completion.

> **PRO TIP:** Use the Host Guarantee sparingly. Personally, I don't use it for anything under $100 as I view these expanses as a cost of doing business. You can bet Airbnb tracks these claims and having many small dollar claims is a drain on Airbnb's limited resources and probably will work against you when you make a larger claim.

How do I submit an Airbnb Host Guarantee payment request?

To submit a Host Guarantee payment request, read through the terms and conditions of the Host Guarantee[58], then contact your guest to notify them of your complaint—often hosts and guests resolve

---

56   www.airbnb.com/help/contact
57   www.airbnb.com/terms/host_guarantee
58   www.airbnb.com/terms/host_guarantee

issues on their own via our Resolution Center. If you and your guest aren't able to come to an agreement, update your case in the Resolution Center accordingly. Gather as much documentation as possible to submit to Airbnb, including photos, receipts, a police report, and any other documentation that proves ownership, damage, or estimates the fair market value of items damaged. Once we receive sufficient information, we will review all documentation and evaluate the payment request under our Host Guarantee terms and conditions.

Should I have a security deposit? How does the Host Guarantee work with the security deposit?

The Host Guarantee does not protect against reasonable wear and tear. The Host Guarantee is designed to protect against rare instances of damage. For smaller, simpler accidents–like a broken glass–a security deposit can be useful for hosts.

What should I do before submitting a payment request?

Contact your guest to notify them of your complaint and try to resolve the issue directly. Oftentimes, hosts and guests can resolve issues on their own.

If you and your guest are unable to come to a resolution, we recommend that you file a police report. A police report is encouraged in all cases and is required for payment requests that exceed $300 USD.

Compile as much documentation as possible to submit with your form. Useful documentation and information that will help process your payment request as quickly as possible include:

- photographs of the damage being claimed
- a police report for any damage that is over $300 USD
- receipts or some alternative evidence of the accurate fair market value or report cost
- proof of ownership
- any other documentation that you feel will be helpful to processing your request

Should I have homeowners or renter's insurance?

The Host Guarantee is not insurance and should not be considered as a replacement or stand-in for homeowners or renter's insurance. Hosts may want to consider independent insurance to cover valuable items like jewelry, artwork, or collectibles which are subject to limited protection under the Host Guarantee. See our Host Guarantee terms[59] for more details.

We strongly encourage all hosts to review and understand the terms of their insurance policy and what it covers and does not cover. Not all insurance plans will cover damage or loss to property caused by a guest who books your space.

How long will it take for my payment request to be processed?

The length of the process will vary depending on the severity of the case, the quality of documentation, and the cooperation of the host and guest. We strive to resolve most cases within a week of submission.

Author Update: I am currently going through a $6,000 claim and have been told it takes a week to a couple months to get assigned an agent. Currently, I have waited two weeks.

Third-Party Airbnb Insurance Providers

You need to do your own due diligence to decide which is best for your situation. There are simply too many variables to offer sound general advice. This decision will also depend on your state. I know some larger insurances provide add-on coverage to existing policies, so may want to also call your existing provider. The below providers have sprung up as a solution for Airbnb hosts. They are not identical. I encourage you to reach out to all of them.

- Proper Insure (www.proper.insure)
- Comet Home (www.comethome.com)
- Slice (slice.is)

---

59   www.airbnb.com/terms/host_guarantee

CHAPTER 38

Q+A with Darren Pettyjohn of Proper Insure

Key Points

▶ Often your existing homeowner's insurance policy has exclusions related to Airbnb.

▶ You need proper business insurance, regardless if you're an owner or renter.

▶ See end of chapter for two questions to ask your current insurance provider to start to understand if you have proper insurance.

A question that comes up often with my Airbnb hosts is insurance. Trying to tackle a behemoth topic such as insurance is a difficult task, yet it's so important. The one consistency I have found in all my years as an Airbnb host, is that you will get different answers from different people, every time you ask a question about insurance for Airbnb Hosts.

Here is a simple question: If I own a second home and half the year I stay there, and the other half the year I rent it out via Airbnb, does my homeowner's insurance cover me for property damage and liability claims?

In preparation for this book, I have asked this question to five different insurance agents, and got five different answers. One agent said it depends on how often you rent it, and another said if you don't tell anyone, you should be fine! Those are not very reassuring answers for such a simple question, especially for someone who business is insurance.

I did some digging and found Darren Pettyjohn, the Co-founder of Proper Insurance, to be the industry expert. Pettyjohn developed a Lloyd's insurance policy specifically tailored for short-term rentals and insures Airbnb properties in all 50 states. I asked him to explain short-term rental insurance as it relates to Airbnb:

Rusteen: Law360 just published an article referencing a California Superior Court case, in which an Airbnb host accuses Travelers of systematically denying property damage claims when any part of a damaged building has been listed for short-term lodging on Airbnb, regardless whether the loss had anything to do with the listing. Are you familiar with this case?

Pettyjohn: Yes. It does not surprise me that large domestic insurers are denying homeowners' claims if they even hear the word Airbnb. An insured person pays a premium for a company to take on risk, and the more the risk, the more the premium. In this case, it not only appears there is a rental exclusion, but I guarantee it had a business activity exclusion as well. Traveler's likely could have denied the claim based on the business activity exclusion, claiming that the host was running a business from their home, which in this case is an Airbnb rental. It's hard for someone to argue an Airbnb rental is not a business.

Rusteen: So any person who rents their property on Airbnb, and has a homeowner's policy, will be denied, regardless whether the claim had anything to do with the actual Airbnb rental?

Pettyjohn: Yes, all standard homeowner's policies have a business activity exclusion, and some form of rental exclusion. However, some carriers are expanding the definition of the rental exclusion and allowing some short-term rentals, capped at a number of days, and typically capped at $10,000 in coverage. They are basically trying to patch a

> • • •
>
> Homeowner's policies are fundamentally wrong from the beginning. They are not written for rentals or for businesses.
>
> • • •

leaky raft, as homeowner's policies are fundamentally wrong from the beginning. They are not written for rentals or for businesses.

> **PRO TIP:** Ask about Fair Rental/Business Income insurance protection which covers lost revenue, sometimes up to two years, if you are unable to continue renting out the property. The good insurers will pay you what you actually earned rather than an average of fair market value (i.e. comparable properties).

Rusteen: What are Airbnb hosts supposed to do?

Pettyjohn: No, they buy business insurance, just like any other business does. Renting out your home for profit is a business. When someone is looking to travel to an area and they have a choice to stay in a hotel, or rent someone's home, you better believe that is business competition. Hotels carry business insurance, so should Airbnb hosts.

Rusteen: What are your thoughts on the insurance providers Slice and Comet as it related to business insurance for Airbnb hosts?

Pettyjohn: They are capitalizing on exactly what we have covered so far, which is a need for business insurance in regards to Airbnb. In my opinion, they are not solving the problem, they are filling in one of many gaps. Let's look at Slice. You pay on average $7/night for property and liability damage that occurs only during the rental period. Their marketing is, only pay for the nights your property is rented. OK, well what happens when a tree falls on your house, during a night in which your property is not rented, and not covered by Slice? This is exactly what happened in the above mentioned case. With Slice, you still must maintain a homeowner's policy, so to my point, it only addresses one of many gaps in a homeowner's policy.

Rusteen: Got it. So I need **a business policy that is written to cover a business, but also written to replace your homeowner's policy?**

Pettyjohn: Yes, 100%. There are essentially three ways you could technically insure a home, you could use homeowner's forms, landlord forms, or business forms. Because Proper uses business forms it gives us the horsepower needed to cover what a homeowner does, and what a landlord does.

Rusteen: Is Proper the only one writing this special policy?

Pettyjohn: No, there are many of carriers who can write a business policy for your home. Proper's coverage is unique in that we put a few special endorsements on our policy, i.e. no limit on theft from a renter, but there are comparable policies.

> **PRO TIP:** The most complete policies will protect against liability, building, contents, and lost income.

Rusteen: What do I do if I want to shop around and compare?

Pettyjohn: You need to get in touch with a local independent insurance agent, preferably one with some time under their belt. Independent agents get appointed with specialty carriers to sell their products, and would be able to service the policy. Be very clear in what you are looking for, i.e. tell them you short-term rent your property on Airbnb, and would like a business policy to replace your current coverage.

Rusteen: Some of my hosts do not own the properties they rent on Airbnb, they actually lease them from the owner, and then manage them on Airbnb as rentals, what do they do for insurance?

Pettyjohn: All the same rules apply, except the re-renter, as we call them, is used to purchase a renter's policy. Proper sells a commercial or business renter's policy, so it works perfectly for the re-renters. Since they do not own the building, they do not need building insurance, they simply need contents, income, and liability insurance, and we add the owner of the property as additionally insured.

Rusteen: What about condos, cabins, and townhouses, how to insure those?

Pettyjohn: Townhomes and cabins are insured the same as single family homes, but condos actually get a commercial or business condo policy. Condo owners carry an HO-6, or homeowner's 6, which is designed for properties in which the owner only insures the walls in, as the association owns and insures the roof and the hallways, etc. The problem with an HO-6 is that the same business activity exclusion applies as in a normal homeowner's policy. The owner of the condo needs business insurance.

Rusteen: Many hosts are putting their Airbnb rentals into an LLC, how does this effect the insurance?

Pettyjohn: An LLC creates an extra layer of protection against a potential liability lawsuit, and it also helps with tax deductions regarding Uncle Sam. For the Proper policy, it has no effect as our policy is a business policy. We name insured's as Sole Props, LLC's, Inc's, LP's, Trusts, and IRA's.

Rusteen: Many of my hosts have mortgages on their properties and don't necessarily want their lenders to know there are renting their properties on Airbnb, how does Proper handle this?

Pettyjohn: Banks have an insurable interest in the property itself, and they need to make certain the property is insured in case of a fire, etc. They need to confirm you carry homeowner's insurance or AKA hazard insurance. The way banks verify insurance is through a standardized document named Evidence of Property Insurance (EPI). On every application, Proper asks if there is a mortgage, and if yes, whose name is on the mortgage, and that is the name that goes on the EPI which goes to the bank for proof of insurance, or escrow payment. I would estimate 40% of our clients carry a mortgage, so this is a non-issue. We never put an LLC or proof of commercial liability on the EPI, as the bank has no interest, nor is it any of their business.

> • • •
>
> An LLC creates an extra layer of protection against a potential liability lawsuit, and it also helps with tax deductions.
>
> • • •

Rusteen: To wrap it up, please give my hosts a few takeaways or action items?

Pettyjohn: My advice to your hosts is to pull out their insurance policy, read it, and ask questions. Airbnb renting is awesome and profitable, but paying for property damage or defending a $1M lawsuit is not. This is the reason people buy insurance, it's a transfer of risk.

When you pull out your policy to read it and call your agent to ask questions, ask these two questions verbatim and get the answers in writing:

1. *If I regularly entrust my property/home to a paying Airbnb guest for a period of less than 30 days, and that guest damages or steals my property, do I have property coverage?*
2. *If I regularly entrust my property/home to a paying Airbnb guest for a period of less than 30 days, and that guest is injured on my property, do I have liability coverage?*

If you are not getting clear answers in writing, then it's time to find a new insurance agent, one that can spend the time to educate you and sell you the proper insurance.

CHAPTER 39

Five Ways to
Contact Airbnb

I f you are trying to find an Airbnb customer service phone number
to call, Airbnb makes your job pretty difficult. You will have to dig
around a bit to get an answer.

This is understandable, as most hosts and guests abuse these phone
lines and create longer wait times for the rest of us. Through some
digging, I found all their urgent support phone numbers listed in one
place. Here they are for your reference:

If your issue is not urgent, try tweeting @Airbnb or @BrianChesky
and they will usually get back to you within a few hours.

Here is what you get from Google if you search 'Airbnb phone number' (current wait times are between 7 and 12 minutes):

Local Urgent Phone Support	✕
United States	+1-415-800-5959
Argentina	+54 11 53 52 78 88
Australia	+61 2 8520 3333
Austria	+43 72 08 83 800
Brazil	+55 21 3958-5800
Chile	+56229380777
China	+86 400-120-9157
Cuba	+1-855-424-7262
Denmark	+45 89 88 20 00
France	+33-184884000
Germany	+49 30 30 80 83 80
Greece	+30 211 1989888
Hong Kong	+852 5808 8888
India	000 800 4405 103
Ireland	+353 1 697 1831
Israel	+972 3 939 9977
Italy	+39-06-99366533
Japan	+81 3 4580 0999
Malaysia	+603 7724 0164
Mexico	+52 55 41 70 43 33
Netherlands	+31 20 52 22 333
New Zealand	+64 4 4880 888
Norway	+47 21 61 16 88
Peru	+51 1 7089777
Poland	+48 22 30 72 000
Portugal	+351 30 880 3888
Puerto Rico	+1 787 945-0222
Russia	+74954658090
Singapore	+65 6622 7306
South Korea	+82 2 6022 2499
Spain	+34 91 123 45 67
Sweden	+46 844 68 12 34
Switzerland	+41 43 50 84 900
Taiwan	+886 2 7743 2436
United Kingdom	+44 203 318 1111

1-855-424-7262

The best toll-free phone number for calling Airbnb
Customer Service is **1-855-424-7262** (Even with this
number, the average wait time is between 7 and 12
minutes). The primary Airbnb mailing address is: 888
Brannan St.

Contact Airbnb Customer Service Quickly - Airbnb Hell
https://www.airbnbhell.com/contact-airbnb/

www.airbnbsecrets.com

The Superhost priority phone number is +1.888.326.5753

As always, you can consult the Help Center[60] or the Community
Center[61].

---

60   www.airbnb.com/help
61   community.withairbnb.com/t5/Community-Center/ct-p/community-center

CHAPTER 40

Useful Airbnb Links

Below is an assortment of useful or interesting Airbnb-related links.

About Us – https://www.airbnb.com/about/about-us
High level facts about Airbnb plus short biographies of the Co-founders. Notice that Brian Chesky's, CEO, is in the middle and has the shortest bio. I find that interesting as usually the CEO would be at the top with the longest bio.

Affiliate Program – https://affiliate.withairbnb.com
Go here to request to partner with Airbnb's host or guest affiliate program.

API – https://goo.gl/vkK3bx
Go here to request access to connect to Airbnb's API.

Airbnb Blog – https://blog.atairbnb.com/
Airbnb Citizen – https://www.airbnbcitizen.com/
The political side of Airbnb with ways to get involved. There's a heat map towards the bottom which highlights the legal situations in numerous cities across the globe.

Airbnb Design – https://airbnb.design/
Learn about Airbnb design and find featured upcoming events. You can also sign up for their newsletter towards the bottom to stay up to date with Airbnb's creative teams.

Airbnb Goods – https://airbnbgoods.com/

Buy Airbnb swag! Small purchases ship to the US only, but if you place a large order then shipping is more flexible.

AirbnbMag – https://airbnbmag.com/
Print magazine you can subscribe to for $15 (6 issues).

Airbnb Open – https://airbnbopen.com/
Dedicated to Airbnb's annual host festival, though not updated at the moment as there was nothing in 2017. However, you can sign up for their newsletter.

Airbnb vs Berlin – http://www.airbnbvsberlin.com/
Berlin is one of the most anti-Airbnb cities in the world. A very impressive and seemingly unbiased review of the effect of Airbnb on Berlin's housing market.

Alumni – https://www.airbnb.com/alumni
If you happen to be an Airbnb alumni, this website helps you stay connected.

Co-Hosting – https://www.airbnb.com/co-hosting
Find a local co-host to help you with your Airbnb.

Community Center – https://goo.gl/rUomwu
Airbnb official forum for Airbnb hosts.

Engineering – http://airbnb.io/
View projects and meet the data science and engineering teams.

Experiences – https://www.airbnb.com/host/experiences
If you have a unique experience to offer travelers visiting your city, apply here.

Facebook – https://www.facebook.com/airbnb
Fast Facts – https://press.atairbnb.com/fast-facts/
Part of Airbnb Newsroom, but with really interesting facts about Airbnb including a timeline of events from 2007.

Guidebooks – https://www.airbnb.com/things-to-do
Based on host identified locations by continent. If your location is on here, add a link to your Airbnb listing!

Host Toolkits – https://www.airbnb-toolkits.com/my_toolkits

Seven courses for Airbnb hosts as prepared by Airbnb.

Medium Blog, Airbnb Design – https://medium.com/airbnb-design

Medium Blog, Airbnb Engineering – https://medium.com/airbnb-engineering

Meetups – https://www.airbnb.com/meetups
A list of worldwide upcoming Airbnb meetups sanctioned by Airbnb.

Neighborhoods – https://www.airbnb.com/locations
Airbnb has written impressive neighborhood guides to 23 locations around the world (I hope they add more!). If your city is on here, be sure to include it in The Neighborhood section of your Airbnb listing.

Neighbors – https://www.airbnb.com/neighbors
Complain here if you think your neighbor is Airbnbing and you have an issue.

Newsroom – https://press.atairbnb.com/
A treasure trove of Airbnb news information.

Night At – https://www.airbnb.com/night-at
Page dedicated to all of Airbnb's Night At promotions.

Niido – http://www.liveniido.com/
Dedicated website to the first of its kind apartment building in Florida branded by Airbnb.

Samara – https://samara.com/
This is the secret projects branch of Airbnb, even located in a totally different office.

Sublets – https://www.airbnb.com/sublets
Specifically created webpage for guests searching for long-term accommodations (1+ months).

Toolkits for Multifamily Properties – https://multifamily.withairbnb.com/index.html
Resources to help Airbnb hosts involved with multifamily properties like HOAs and apartment buildings. Also, information on their Friendly Buildings Program.

Vimeo – https://vimeo.com/airbnb
Videos by Airbnb, only 805 subscribers, show some love!

YouTube – https://www.youtube.com/user/Airbnb
Almost 100k subscribers, but still highly underrated. Lots of valuable and entertaining content on here.

Final Notes

I truly hope that you received immense value from reading this book. I have a request and an offer. I want to offer you the ability to get in touch with me, you can do so by emailing Danny@OptimizeMyAirbnb.com. Praise, criticism, introducing me to your Airbnb related business, it's all welcomed. I want to request that you leave me a book review on the platform you used to purchase this book. Just as reviews significantly help your Airbnb, they significantly help me.

Be sure to check my blog for updated content: www.OptimizeMyAirbnb.com/Blog.

Follow me on:

- **Instagram:** www.instagram.com/optimizemyairbnb
- **Facebook:** www.facebook.com/optimizemyairbnb
- **Twitter:** www.twitter.com/OptimizeAirbnb
- **YouTube:** Search for OptimizeMyAirbnb

You can find relevant information as it relates to the book on the dedicated website: www.OptimizeYourAirbnb.com.

If you would like personalized help, please purchase an Airbnb Listing Optimization Report or schedule a phone call with me at www.OptimizeMyAirbnb.com/additional-airbnb-optimization.